THE GERMAN CANADIAN MOSAIC TODAY AND YESTERDAY

Identities, Roots, and Heritage

Gerhard P. Bassler

German-Canadian Congress

Ottawa, 1991

ISBN: 0-9695486-0-5

The financial assistance of the Government of Canada is gratefully acknowledged.

The author welcomes any suggestions for revision and encourages readers to draw his attention to unpublished documents, such as immigration and church records, diaries, letters, and photographs.

Dr. Gerhard P. Bassler, Department of History, Memorial University of Newfoundland, St. John's, Newfoundland, Canada A1C 5S7

Tel: 709-737-7920/8420 Fax: 709-737-4569

E-mail: gbassler@kean.ucs.mun.ca

*To a truer understanding of
Canada's past and present*

CONTENTS

CONTENTS

CONTENTS

CONTENTS

CONTENTS

CONTENTS

INTRODUCTION

The original impulse for this book came from Dietrich Kiesewalter, Ottawa. As General Secretary of the newly launched German-Canadian Congress in 1985, he pointed to the dire need for an easily comprehensible, concise survey of German-Canadian history, written from a national perspective and presenting the latest historical scholarship. The book is intended as (1) a frame of reference for teachers in German heritage language schools, (2) a possible instructional supplement in Canadian schools and university undergraduate courses, and (3) an historical overview for anyone interested in the history of German Canadians.

This book, therefore, serves students and teachers, laymen and scholars, members and non-members of the German-Canadian ethnis group - in other words, all those looking for a comprehensive view of the history of Canada's people of German background. By "German" are meant German-speaking immigrants and those of their descendants who acknowledged their German cultural roots, regardless of geographic origin and linguistic assimilation. Their heritage is, unfortunately, not well known either among themselves or among Canadians in general. Moreover, their experiences and contributions have gone largely unacknowledged in the standard works on Canadian history. Readers of this book may be surprised to discover that people of German-speaking background form Canada's largest and oldest non-French, non-British, and non-native ethnic group, that their presence

as pioneers can be traced in every region of the country, and
the significance of their contributions to Canada's growth is
visible in every phase of Canadian history. Why this heritage
has generally remained obscure is an integral aspect of the
text.

This book intends not just to present facts, but also to give
food for thought. It is designed to provoke classroom
discussion and inquiries and, it is hoped, further research. The
aim is to provide a structured and critical guide through
nearly four centuries of history. The text organizes German-
Canadian history into thirty chapters identifying the main
historical episodes and the German-speaking groups who
shaped or were shaped by them.

The thirty chapters are further divided into five groups of
between four and seven consecutive and thematically coherent
topics. Each group of topics represents one of five major
cycles of German-speaking migration to Canada, and, within
each cycle, the migration is traced to its earliest beginnings:
(1) the post-World War II migration, (2) the interwar period,
(3) the migration between Confederation and World War I,
(4) the migration between the American Revolution and
Confederation (1870), and (5) the pre-Revolutionary migration dating as far back as the Norse in A.D. 1000. The
intention of this device is to give readers a feeling for the
main watersheds in German-Canadian migration and ethnic
history, as well as for the interaction among different
immigrant generations, and the problems resulting from
different degrees of assimilation.

The approach is based on the migration process and
experience. Individual immigrants experience -- as distinct
phases of their lives -- the circumstances of emigration from
their country of birth, immigration to Canada, settlement,
and, finally, adjustment. The history of Canada's Germans
may be similarly conceived of as consisting of several major
waves of immigration. Each wave has a different combination
of origins, conditions of immigration, opportunities for
settlement, and problems of adjustment. Just as the particular
experiences of individual immigrants are traceable to their
roots, so the unique experiences of different generations of
immigrants need to be traced to their geographic and cultural

origins in order to become fully comprehensible.

Since tracing roots in the search for one's identity means going back, this historical survey reverses the chronological order by moving from the present to the past. While this may at first appear to be confusing for some who consider history as a forward chronological sequence of events, it has the advantage of requiring no prior background information on the part of the reader. Whatever background is needed is explained in the process of going back. Instead of treading uncertainly from the distant unknown past into the known present, the reader goes one analyzed step at a time connecting the unknown past with an understood link to the present. By thus drawing students and teachers into a systematic endeavour to trace the roots of the mosaic of German-Canadian groups and to explore the origins of their culture, the study of German-Canadian history becomes virtually self-explanatory and personally relevant.

A number of people merit recognition for their assistance. Edith Kuntz deserves credit for her untiring efforts to collect a large variety of documents. Ideas and materials were contributed by my colleagues Karin Gürttler, Peter Liddell, Manfred Prokop, Dieter Roger, and Arthur Grenke, and by Leslie Angele from the Deutsche Sprachschule Concordia Saskatoon Inc. My colleague Robert Keyserlingk offered beneficial comments. I am grateful for Bernice Link's proofreading assistance. The timely completion of this project is above all indebted to the indispensable editorial support of my wife, Tonya Kurt Bassler.

St. John's, Newfoundland,

May 1991

CHAPTER I

GERMAN CANADIANS TODAY

1. Visible contributions
2. The multicultural context
3. The historical record
4. Shadows of the past

Visible contributions

The contributions of German Canadians to the life of
Canada are noticeable on many levels and in many ways.
Sheer numbers alone give German Canadians an important
place in Canadian history and society. In the 1981 Census, 1.2
million Canadians or 5 percent of the population reported
their ethnic origin to be German. This means they constitute
Canada's third largest ethnic group, after the British and the
French. Their significance in the history of settlement is
indicated by numerous German place names across Canada.
Their traditions have woven many brilliant threads into the
rich tapestry of Canadian society, as Prime Minister Pierre
Eliot Trudeau put it metaphorically in 1973.

People of German-speaking descent take credit for various
contributions to the cultural heritage shared by all Canadians,
ranging from the art of wine growing and beer brewing to the
Oktoberfest celebration, the Easter bunny tradition, and the
decorated Christmas tree. Their image is that of a people who
work hard but also cultivate *Gemütlichkeit* in the home and
in public. They are known for popularizing *Karneval* fun,
brass band music, folk festivals, and instrumental and singing
performances. For two centuries, German-Canadian musicians
have pioneered the professional cultivation of music in
Canada, whether in the form of band music, opera performances, philharmonic societies, or choir competitions. Simi-

larly, over more than two centuries, German settlers from eastern to western Canada have contributed an impressive and important body of folk art, characterized by art critic Michael Bird as "a legacy of excellence, joy in creation, and respect for tradition."

In recent years, German Canadians have been found not only among the country's most distinguished musical directors (Hermann Geiger-Torel, Günther Herbig, Heinz Unger), artists (Herbert Siebner, Carl Rungius, Hugo Wüthrich, Lutz Haufschild, Almuth Lütkenhaus), writers (Henry Kreisel, Frederick Philip Grove), architects (Eberhard Zeidler, Cornelia Oberlander, Martin Bergen), and scientists (Nobel Prize winner Gerhard Herzberg and Canadarm developer Klaus Wagner-Bartak), but also among the most prominent entrepreneurs (the Eppich brothers, Frank Stronach, Ulrich Freybe), as well as among the most notorious criminals (Helmuth Buxbaum), and politically infamous prostitutes (Gerda Munsinger). Just as visible are the success stories of countless ordinary German-speaking post-World War II immigrants rising from rags to riches. Their invaluable expertise as professionals, businessmen, farmers, or skilled workers constitutes a vital element in the continuing growth and prosperity of the nation.

German Canadians have also been prominent in recent federal politics where they have served in the capacity of governor general (Ed Schreyer), prime minister (John Diefenbaker), federal ministers (Otto Lang, Otto Jellinek, Frank Oberle, Jake Epp), and federal opposition critics (Benno Friesen, Ernie Epp). Although three fathers of Confederation were of German descent -- Sir Charles Tupper (Nova Scotia), William Henry Steeves, and Charles Fisher (both New Brunswick) -- German Canadians have traditionally not been as active in politics as in other domains of life.

The multicultural context

Canada has been built by immigrants from many lands and by the descendants of these immigrants. Its present population, therefore, claims a great variety of ethnic descent, cultural backgrounds, and national origins. For instance, some of these Canadians are very recent arrivals like the Tamils, some are concentrated in urban areas like the Italians and Portuguese, some in rural areas like the Russian Doukhobors, some in the prairies like the Ukrainians, and some on the west coast like the Japanese. Census figures show that people claiming German descent are one of the largest ethnic groups in every part of Canada, from coast to coast. They are represented equally in rural and urban regions. In eastern Canada they constitute the third largest ethnic group, exceeded only by those who claim British and French descent. In western Canada, people claiming German descent form the largest group after the British. In terms of its size and geographic dispersal, the position of the German element in the multicultural mosaic of Canadian society is thus comparable only to that of the British.

The historical role of German Canadians is also significant because from the time we have data on the ethnic composition of Canadian society they have always been among Canada's three largest and most important immigrant groups. The cultural variety and the way of life that we identify as the essence of Canada today are the legacy of successive generations of European settlers. The first settlers came from French, English, and German-speaking areas of western Europe. In the 19th century they were joined by settlers from the remaining parts of northern, eastern, and southern Europe. French, English, and German-speaking settlers have passed on their customs to the native Indians and Inuit and have laid the foundations for a new culture to be shared with native peoples and non-European immigrants in Canada. Nevertheless, only a minority of the earlier generations of German-speaking immigrants have maintained their linguistic heritage until this day, while the majority have become assimilated into Canada's anglophone and francophone societies. The Canadian Census, however, reveals that the memory of German roots is still alive among many linguistically assimilated German immigrants.

The historical record

German Canadians pride themselves on a permanent presence of more than three centuries in this country. The

achievements of German-speaking pioneers in the opening up
and development of large parts of Nova Scotia, Ontario, the
Prairies, and British Columbia are irrefutable historical facts.
In the English-French wars for the control of North America,
Germans fought on both sides, and German troops were
indispensable in the defence of British North America against
the threats of the American Revolution. A large number of
the Loyalists, who are honoured as the founders of Canada,
were actually of German origin.

Because of their record, Germans might properly be
considered as co-founders of Canada. The visible and invisible
monuments of their work reveal that successive waves of
German-speaking immigrants have shown remarkable adaptability to Canada's unique variety of challenges, be it as
missionaries, fishermen, boatbuilders, farmers, skilled workers,
artisans, businessmen, entrepreneurs, professionals, or artists.
A record of loyalty to the Crown, economic success, and the
British perception of cultural proximity and racial compatibi-
lity had caused Germans to be ranked among Canada's
preferred settlers next to the British, except for the period
during and immediately following the two world wars. The
attention devoted by historical scholars and the Canadian
public to the contributions made by settlers of German-
speaking origin to Canada's growth and fortunes appears,
however, to have been in inverse relationship to the historic
importance of these settlers.

Shadows of the past

One of the chief reasons German Canadians have not been
accorded the historical recognition due them has to do with
the strong passions aroused by the two world wars. After 1914
and again after 1939, people of German-speaking background
were judged no longer by their contributions to Canada, but
by events in Europe. Suspected of ties with Germany and
Austria -- Canada's opponents in both recent world wars --
German Canadians were treated as enemy aliens in their own
country. Some of Canada's towns founded and named by
German immigrants prior to World War I, such as Berlin,
Coblenz, Waldorf, Prussia, and Düsseldorf, were renamed

Kitchener, Cavell, Béthune, Leader, and Freedom. Even second- and third-generation German Canadians have been stigmatized and stereotyped. Their historic record has been generally belittled, distorted, or ignored by Canadian historians and the public.

Recovery from the status of pariahs has been slow for German Canadians since World War II, owing perhaps to a resurging public consciousness in the 1970's and 1980's of the atrocities, especially the Jewish Holocaust, committed by the Nazi regime in Germany. In connection with the public campaign in the late 1980s to identify and prosecute surviving Nazi war criminals in Canada (i.e., those who had murdered civilians during World War II) considerable publicity was given to a small group of German-Canadian agitators in Toronto who denounced the irrefutable evidence of the Holocaust. These Holocaust deniers, as well as allegations that large numbers of Nazi war criminals were hiding among Canada's post-World War II immigrants, have harmed the German-Canadian image by associating today's German Canadians with the most objectionable aspects of recent German history.

CHAPTER II

THE GERMAN-CANADIAN MOSAIC

1. Geographic roots
2. National origins
3. Denominations
4. Generations

The geographic roots of German Canadians

The various areas known as Germany in recent history are not the homelands of most German Canadians. Rather, they came with different social, denominational, and cultural backgrounds from many lands in Europe and the Americas. Canada's German community may be characterized as one of the world's most colourful mosaics of origins, denominations, and cultural adaptations gathered together anywhere under the label of German. German-speaking Canadians thus seem to have little in common except their language; yet the German language and the cultural heritage and traditions that are part of it give them a feeling of shared identity and a sense of community, which does not always disappear even with linguistic assimilation.

Between one half and two thirds of today's German Canadians trace their roots to eastern Europe, where their ancestors migrated from Germany centuries ago in response to the calls for pioneer farmers and colonists from Bohemian (Czech), Polish, Austrian, Hungarian, and Russian monarchs. Their settlements could be found all over eastern Europe, from the Baltic coast to the Ukrainian shore of the Black Sea, from Polish Volhynia to the (now Yugoslavian) Batschka and Banat, and from the (now Czech) Sudetenland and the Romanian province of Transylvania to the Volga River on the Asian frontier of Europe. They brought with them to Canada the German language and culture, as well as a rural lifestyle and valuable skills in pioneer farming, which they had preserved in their east European colonies from the time of their ancestors' emigration from Germany. Their cultural baggage often also included elements of the rural non-German cultures of their east European environments, such as the Russian courtyard style among buildings of the Volga German immigrants.

German Americans and German Swiss pioneered some of the earliest settlements in eastern and western Canada. German Americans have traditionally formed up to twenty per cent of Canada's German community; Germans from Switzerland, Latin America, and Australia less than five per cent. The more urbanized Germans from Germany seldom made up even a quarter of Canada's German-speaking immigrants. In contrast to the other German-speaking immigrants, they preferred the urban life of Kitchener, Toronto, Winnipeg, and Vancouver to the challenges of pioneer farming.

National origins

Due to their disparate geographic roots, German Canadians, with the possible exception of the Swiss, have never attributed much significance to their national origins. Among the ordinary people of central and eastern Europe, nationalism did not become a popular sentiment until the end of the 19th century. The multinational and anti-democratic structure of the Austro-Hungarian Empire, the denial of national self-determination to the small post-World War I Republic of Austria, and its union with Germany from 1938 to 1945, delayed the development of a distinct national identity among German Austrians until the 1950's. Germans from eastern Europe, known as *Volksdeutsche* since the 1930's, did not want to be labelled as Russians, Hungarians, Poles, etc., any more than they cared to be associated with the modern German nation state. Until World War I even German immigrants from Germany, also known as *Reichsdeutsche*, frequently preferred to be identified by their region, for example, as Bavarians, Swabians, Palatines, and Saxons, rather than as German nationals.

In the names of their secular clubs organized after the two

world wars -- such as those of the *Donauschwaben*, the
Siebenbürger Sachsen (Transylvania Saxons), the *Sudeten
Klub*, the *Bayern Klub*, and the *Berliner Klub*, *Reichsdeutsche*
and *Volksdeutsche* immigrants manifest a continued allegiance to fellowship based on their common geographic
region or place of origin, rather than their country of
emigration and former residence. Of course, Swiss, Austrian,
and German clubs can be found in major Canadian cities
today. But one may also find that among Swiss, Austrians, and
natives of Germany allegiance to one all-embracing German
Kulturnation often overrides loyalty to an Austrian, Swiss or
German nationality, as the life and works of the eminent
Swiss Canadian author and writer Hermann Boeschenstein
demonstrates. The shared cultural heritage enables German-
speaking Canadians from all parts of Europe to interact as
one community.

Denominations

   Neither geographic roots nor nationalist sentiment, however,
offered as decisive a criterion for structuring the German-
Canadian community as denominational affiliation. In the
18th, 19th, and early 20th centuries the church had been the
only vehicle of social and cultural organization for most
German immigrants in the Old World, and it continued to be
so in the new pioneer environment of Canada. An examination of German settlement patterns in Canada reveals that
German-speaking immigrants of the same denominational
background desired to settle together regardless of their
former homelands or places of origin. Thus, Mennonites are
known to have pioneered the largest and most viable German
settlements in eastern and western Canada, just as Catholics,
Lutherans, Baptists, Reformed, and Moravians located in
specific places.

   Religion has united as well as divided German Canadians in
more than one way. It has hindered intimate social interaction
among members of different churches and foiled inter-
denominational efforts to defend common German-Canadian
cultural-political interests. On the other hand, religious
separation was also responsible for the survival of the German
language and culture for several generations among certain

denominations, such as the Hutterites and Old Order Mennonites. It has also assigned Mennonites a leading cultural role among German Canadians.

The largest denominational groups among German Canadians are Lutherans, followed by Mennonites and Catholics. Mennonites, as well as Lutherans, are again subdivided into a number of feuding orthodox and reformist branches. Mennonites are, furthermore, separated into Swiss and Russian Mennonites, according to their different homelands, from which they brought with them such different German linguistic patterns as the Swabian-Palatine dialect and Low German. One of the most orthodox Mennonite groups is the Amish, who reject all modern conveniences in their homes and private lives. Another is the Hutterites, who live on communal farms and practice a kind of Christian communism. The Lutheran, Mennonite, Reformed, and Moravian creeds are typical German forms of Protestantism and were introduced to Canada by the first German Protestant settlers in the mid-18th century (see chapters XXIV to XXVIII).

Most Jewish Canadians of German-speaking background identify with the Jewish ethnic group. A minority of the German-speaking Jews fleeing from persecution in Europe have endeavoured to maintain an ethno-religious identity of their own.

Generations

A further division among German Canadians occurs between the new immigrants, the partially assimilated second or third generation of earlier immigrants and the linguistically fully assimilated descendants of the pioneer generation. In areas of traditional German settlement, such as Lunenburg (Nova Scotia), Kitchener-Waterloo (Ontario), and St. Peter's Colony (Saskatchewan), one may find recent German immigrants living side by side with the children of immigrants from the 1920's as well as the offspring of Germans who arrived in the 19th or even 18th centuries. One may find that, even when the descendants of earlier generations of immigrants have lost the ability to speak German, they may have retained not only the memory of their roots, but also residues of their German ancestors' culture, such as preferences for certain foods or old traditions of celebrating Christmas. Studies have shown that, since the 18th century, German Canadians in the second generation have retained only a moderate and reluctant fluency in German (unless they are Mennonites or Hutterites), and in the third generation the ability to speak German has usually been lost. A desire for social acceptance and upward mobility and the high proportion of marriages with members of non-German groups have been the main causes for Canadian-born children and grandchildren of German-speaking immigrants to distance themselves from their ancestral heritage and German image.

Communication difficulties, however, often arise even between newcomers and old-established German Canadians who have retained the ability to speak German in the second or third generation of residence in Canada. Although both the new and the long-established German Canadians might speak the same German dialect from the same European homelands, their frames of reference can be incomprehensible to each other. Not only have the long- established German Canadians become more or less Canadianized, but their perspectives and perceptions of German culture tended to stagnate at their time of immigration. A good example of this dilemma is provided by three generations of Mennonite immigrants from Russia: the pre-World War I *Kanadier,* the post-World War I *Russländer,* and the post-World War II Mennonite refugees (see chapter XI).

Despite their large numbers, today's Canadians of German background have become the silent or hidden ethnic group in Canadian society. They are among Canada's most Canadianized residents and are usually distinguishable from other Canadians only by their names. They attest to the fact that Canada's German immigrant culture has, with few but significant exceptions, been confined to the generation of the newcomers. Throughout Canadian history, waves of German immigrants have readily assimilated into the anglophone and francophone host societies.

CHAPTER III

THE ADJUSTMENT OF POST-WORLD WAR II IMMIGRANTS

1. Problems and challenges of adaptation
2. National ethnic organizations
3. Social clubs
4. Churches

Problems and challenges of adaptation

The generation of the post-World War II immigrants represents the dominant element in the German-Canadian community today. Anyone taking notice of the problems and achievements of these immigrants will realize that they have faced unique challenges in Canada. The high levels of economic security and prosperity enjoyed among most present-day German Canadians parallel the spectacular economic resurgence of West Germany and Austria. Their economic well-being is the fruit of their determination to overcome with hard work the negative experiences of the past.

Occupational adjustment was often a painful process for the well-educated German-speaking newcomers, many of whom were initially forced to find immediate employment as farm labourers in the West or as loggers in the North in order to survive. In the 1950's and 1960's trades unions, professional associations, and educational institutions frequently excluded German immigrants from membership; at the same time, employers paid them lower wages than native employees earned. What assured the ultimate successful economic integration of German-speaking immigrants was the expertise and the work ethic brought by them. Endowed with the qualifications of skilled workers, technicians, and professionals, they were able to meet a great demand for specialized training in the rapidly expanding Canadian postwar economy.

Social and psychological adjustment has posed no less

formidable a challenge to these immigrants and has not always succeeded as smoothly as their economic integration. Residues of a deep anti-German sentiment in British Canada have created many obstacles to the full social integration of German Canadians despite their welcome contributions to Canada's postwar economic development. Until the 1960's it was virtually impossible for German Canadians to be elected to public office on any level of government. They were stereotyped in the media and at their place of work and their children were stigmatized in school. Even fully assimilated fourth-generation German Canadians like John Diefenbaker, Prime Minister of Canada from 1957 to 1963, viewed their German names as a serious handicap in politics and had to renounce their German roots to be politically successful.

The postwar generation responded to these problems in two ways. The majority aspired to full linguistic and cultural assimilation in the first generation and sought to become the invisible ethnic group. A minority, eager to preserve their German heritage, devoted themselves to maintaining a world of ethnic organizations, social clubs, educational institutions, cultural events, and churches in areas where pre-World War II German-speaking immigrants had laid the foundations for such associations. This visible world of German-Canadian organizations and activities, viewed as the manifestation of German-Canadian ethnocultural life today, serves a threefold purpose: It is, on the one hand, a supportive attempt to ease the newcomer's adaptation and adjustment to the New World. On the other hand, it represents a deliberate effort to reconstitute a piece of the Old World by a generation whose pattern of socialization and outlook was shaped in the Old World and who, as first-generation immigrants, will never experience complete integration into Canadian life. Thirdly, it constitutes an undertaking through which a group of immigrants dedicated to the preservation of their linguistic and cultural heritage hope to pass on this heritage to their offspring.

National ethnic organizations

One of the first nationwide German-speaking secular associations formed after the Second World War was the

Trans-Canada Alliance of German-Canadians. Its main objective has been to further the German cultural cause from coast to coast by supporting and coordinating German-language instruction through a network of so-called Saturday schools *(Sonnabendschulen)*. In the larger cities from Ontario to British Columbia, local German-speaking businesspeople and entrepreneurs have formed German-Canadian Business and Professional Associations to further their special economic interests. Postwar immigrants from the major German-speaking regions of Europe (Russia, the Baltic, Transylvania, the Danube, the Sudeten, Austria, and Switzerland) have established so-called *Landsmannschaften* on the national level to maintain their unique ethnocultural and social identity. The Historical Society of Mecklenburg-Upper Canada and the German-Canadian Historical Association draw attention to monuments of the past and promote the study of the cultural heritage of German Canadians. The German-Canadian Congress, founded in 1984 as the national umbrella organization for Canadians of ethnic German descent, has assumed the advocacy role for the German-Canadian community's national political and cultural interests within the context of official multiculturalism.

Social clubs

In the central Canadian areas of traditional German settlement (Kitchener-Waterloo, Windsor, Hamilton, Toronto, and Ottawa), as well as in the urban areas of the West (Winnipeg, Regina, Saskatoon, Edmonton, Calgary, and Vancouver), all kinds of local secular clubs are cultivating fellowship among German-speaking immigrants. The clubs promote one or more activities, such as singing, dancing, shooting and hunting, card playing, sports, instrumental music, eating, drinking, and relief aid. The most common rallying cry is the preservation of the customs and traditions known and practiced by the immigrants in their European places of origin. This purpose is often reflected in the names of these clubs, such as *Bayrischer Freizeit Club* (Toronto) and *Schuhplattlergruppe "Alpenland"* (Montreal). Most offer their members a variety of services and entertainment ranging from Mardi Gras celebrations and folk festivals to educational programs and material support. By thus providing a comfortable German cultural environment for the entire family of the immigrant, these clubs nourish the hope that this heritage will be passed on to the children of the immigrants.

Churches

While secular clubs exist only in certain parts of Canada, churches and denominational associations have played an active role in facilitating the adjustment of the postwar immigrant across the entire country, in urban as well as in rural areas. In the 1950s the Mennonite, Lutheran, Catholic, and Baptist churches established the most comprehensive service structure on a national and international scope. They attempted to provide for every need of German-speaking immigrants, from arranging their passage from overseas to looking after their educational, health, and welfare problems. In the metropolitan areas, a few Lutheran, Catholic, and Baptist churches continue to provide services and fellowship in German, but the shrinking demand for their services and the secularization of Canadian society has reduced the churches' role mainly to serving the spiritual needs of their members.

CHAPTER IV

THE IMMIGRATION OF THE 1950's

1. Canadian immigration policy
2. The push and pull of mass migration
3. Hopes and fears of the immigrants
4. First experiences in Canada

Canadian immigration policy

At least two thirds of the entire post-World War II generation of German-Canadian newcomers arrived in the 1950's. These one quarter of a million German-speaking immigrants formed twenty per cent of Canada's total immigration in that decade and constituted a greater mass influx of Germans than Canada had ever experienced before. Ethnic German immigration jumped from 5,800 in 1950 to 32,400 in 1951 when Canadian immigrants of German origin were the largest ethnic group and exceeded those of British origin by 1,000. German immigration peaked in 1953 with 39,000 and dropped to 12,000 by 1960. Throughout the 1960's the figure for immigrants of German origin fluctuated well below 10,000 and in the 1970's below 5,000.

The influx of the 1950's was made possible because in September 1950 the federal government removed the German enemy alien prohibition in effect for the previous eleven years and began the new policy of admitting German nationals on the same basis as the nationals of other countries. Not only were Germans of all backgrounds (with the exception of those classified as Nazi war criminals and those identified as Communists) permitted to enter Canada, but Germans were now included among the Canadian government's preferred immigrants.

Preferred status was based on three factors that determined Canadian immigration policy until 1957. First, Canada's so-called "absorptive capacity" for immigrants was to be determined by the domestic demand for labour. Since the booming postwar economy experienced an acute labour shortage, the Canadian government was eager to recruit suitable foreign labour, primarily for agricultural, logging, and mining industries, but also for manufacturing industries where skills were domestically unavailable. Second, in its search for a "suitable" source of foreign labour, the government first turned to those classified as "most preferred countries" on the basis of national-racial criteria. These criteria were based on the current ethnic composition of the Canadian population and gave priority to British, Scandinavian, and West European -- including German -- immigrants over all others. This immigration policy encouraged the sponsorship of many Germans by Canadian relatives, as well as by Canadian employers eager to obtain German skilled and unskilled employees. Third, Canadian government records leave no doubt that the reputation of Germans as excellent settlers was well established and that their professional, technical, and industrial skills were viewed as valuable assets to the national economy.

The push and pull of mass migration

Canadian immigration policy was only one among a number of reasons for the German mass migration to Canada in the 1950's. Some factors made Germans eager to emigrate from Europe while other factors drew them to Canada. Major push factors were the unsettled economic, social, and political conditions in central Europe in the early 1950's, i.e., unemployment due to the large number of refugees waiting to be integrated into the war-ravaged and dislocated economy and the deep fear of a communist advance into western Europe in the wake of the Korean War. Among the pull factors were thousands of German Canadians willing to sponsor the immigration of relatives from Europe, the opportunities for instant employment in the expanding Canadian economy, and the prospect of personal security in a prosperous and neutral land untouched by war and assured of a great future. The so-called "Assisted Passage Loan Scheme" introduced in 1950, added further to the attractions of immigrating to Canada. With it, Canada offered interest-free loans to immigrants whose skills were needed; from 1955 on their families were also eligible for the loans. The loans provided for travel costs and required repayment within 25 months after arrival.

Changing push and pull forces also help to explain the decline of German-speaking immigration to Canada at the end of the 1950's. By then, Germany and Austria were experiencing such a spectacular economic recovery that they were attracting a growing number of foreign "guest workers" to meet their own labour shortage, while Canada was suffering from increasing unemployment. By the late 1960's an actual return migration of German immigrants from Canada to Europe was beginning in response to the reversal of push and pull forces.

Hopes and fears of the immigrants

As far as their occupation and family status were concerned, approximately half of the immigrants could be classified as blue collar workers and half were dependents. A high proportion of the immigrants listed as German by ethnic origin were refugees. However, Canadian statistical data about German immigration do not distinguish between natives of West Germany and displaced Germans from the East, such as refugees from the Soviet zone of Germany, expellees driven from those parts of Germany annexed by Poland and the Soviet Union, and *Volksdeutsche* who had fled from their east European homelands to West Germany. In the early 1950's one fifth of the population of West Germany consisted of refugees who had lost everything. West Germany was not their homeland. There they had to compete for jobs with local residents and were not always accepted. In addition, Germans from the rural areas of the East had difficulties adjusting to the highly urbanized life of West Germany.

Consequently, many refugees wanted to leave the Europe of their ordeals behind them for good and start a new life in North America. Residents of Germany and Austria saw Canada as the land of the future and the land of unlimited opportunities. Many Germans, who had suffered greatly during and after the war and who feared being drawn into

another impending war in central Europe, believed that
Canada could provide a better future for their children.
Germans and Austrians had been deprived of the opportunity
to travel for more than a decade, and a large number of them
simply wanted to see the world, work abroad for awhile, learn
English, and decide later whether they should remain abroad
or return.

First experiences in Canada

In the 1950's most immigrants arrived in Canada by boat. All
had been subjected overseas to a meticulous process of
medical, occupational, and security screening and many had
received their visas only after long delays. Leaving Germany
from Bremerhaven or Hamburg in one of the old emigrants'
ships, and landing in Halifax, Quebec City, or Montreal was a
dramatic event for them. After celebrating their departure
from the Old World, the immigrants had time to prepare
themselves psychologically for the new beginning. Most knew
little or no English and anticipated Canada to be a land of
milk and honey. Except for a few who had friends or relatives
awaiting them in Canada or those who had been contracted as
skilled workers, the majority were on their own, scrambling
for survival in an unknown world. This meant working for
minimum pay in the least attractive jobs, such as in the sugar
beet fields of Alberta or the mines or logging camps of
northern Ontario. Here they had to endure the most primitive
living conditions and frequently also encountered the anti-
foreign prejudice of their unskilled native co-workers. The
realization of the geographic size of the country and the
relative backwardness of its vast semi-developed regions added
to the trauma of isolation and abandonment. The test of a
severe culture shock was therefore one of the most basic first
experiences that the immigrants of the 1950's had to pass on
the road to successful adaptation.

CHAPTER V

THE ADMISSION OF REFUGEES AND DISPLACED PERSONS 1945-1950

1. Canada's post-World War II refugee policy
2. The Canadian Christian Council for the Resettlement of Refugees (CCCRR)
3. The rescue of the Mennonite refugees from Russia
4. The exclusion of German nationals

Canada's post-World War II refugee policy

After the end of the Second World War in 1945, Canada did not reopen her gates to any immigrants until 1947. The only exception was made for 4,000 Polish ex-servicemen who did not want to return to communist Poland from Britain. These were allowed in with the argument that they were to take over the farm chores assigned to many of the 35,000 German POWs held in Canada during the war. The German POWs were sent back to Germany in 1946. Provisions for the resettlement of displaced and homeless persons from Europe were introduced as part of Canada's new immigration policy proclaimed by Prime Minister Mackenzie King in May 1947. *Volksdeutsche* refugees (who were not German nationals) were included from the beginning in this new policy, which enabled 21,000 of them to enter by September 1950. This was not self-evident, since the charter members (including Canada) of the International Refugee Organization (IRO) had agreed from the outset to exclude all refugees of German ethnic origin from its mandate and care.

In spite of Canada's extension of the state of war with Germany until July 1951 and the classification of German nationals as "prohibited enemy aliens" until September 1950, the Canadian government did more to respond to the needs of German-speaking refugees at the end of World War II than other major immigrant receiving countries. Canada's refugee policy benefitted ethnic German refugees in three ways: First, it enabled their sponsorship by close relatives residing in Canada. Second, it extended the resettlement and employment schemes reserved for displaced persons (DPs) under the mandate of the IRO to a certain group of ethnic German refugees, and, third, it encouraged the foundation of an official Canadian refugee resettlement agency specifically designed for a large class of German-speaking refugees who were excluded from the care of IRO.

The Canadian Christian Council for the Resettlement of Refugees (CCCRR)

The Canadian agency making the most significant contribution to German immigration after 1947 was the CCCRR. By 1950 it had arranged the immigration of 15,000 German-speaking immigrants to Canada, and by 1953 a total of 30,000. The CCCRR was founded in Ottawa in June 1947 with the support of the Canadian government by representatives of the Canadian Lutheran, Catholic, Mennonite, and Baptist churches, and the Sudeten Germans. Based on the model of the IRO (whose mandate excluded all Germans), it prepared and presented eligible prospective German immigrants to the Canadian government screening teams in Europe. Those ineligible for the IRO mandate thus covered were (1) employable *Volksdeutsche* in good health who had not assumed German citizenship voluntarily, (2) German war brides of Canadian servicemen, and (3) a clearly defined class of close relatives of Canadians. Without IRO's or CCCRR's thorough preparation, which included documentation, X-ray examination, blood tests, and relocation to an assembly camp, no immigrants could proceed to Canada.

Confronted on the first day of its operations with more than 10,000 applications from German Canadians eager to sponsor close relatives, a shortage of shipping facilities, and an inexperienced staff of clergymen, the CCCRR had to overcome staggering problems. Only a monthly grant of $10,000 from the Canadian government and the refitting and chartering of the S.S. *Beaverbrae* with a carrying capacity of almost 800 people enabled the CCCRR to function adequately. Since the United States did not accept *volksdeutsche* refugees until 1949, the CCCRR was the only North American agency to which prospective immigrants could turn, and there were more than ten million German-speaking refugees crowded together in occupied Europe between 1945 and 1950.

The rescue of the Mennonite refugees from Russia

Aside from the CCCRR, only the Canadian Mennonites, particularly those who had immigrated after the First World War, managed to bring *Volksdeutsche* to Canada as early as 1947. A particularly spectacular achievement was the successful rescue by Canada's *Russländer* Mennonites of fellow Mennonites displaced from the Soviet Union. Because of their own refugee experience, the *Russländer* sympathized greatly with the plight of German-speaking refugees and expellees. Desperate to prevent the forced repatriation to Soviet Asia of the 10,000 Mennonite refugees who had managed to flee to the western zones of Germany, Canadian Mennonite representatives sought the protection and assistance of the IRO by registering the *volksdeutsche* Mennonites according to their denominational origin as displaced persons of Dutch descent (see chapter XXIV, part 3). The Canadian *Russländer*, who formed the largest group of surviving western relatives of these 10,000 refugees, planned to bring them all to Canada. Sympathetic IRO and Canadian government officials accepted the evidence that the Mennonites had not left the Ukraine voluntarily, that they were not *volksdeutsch* but of Dutch origin, and that they had not served in the German army or any branch of the Nazi Party. By September 1950, with the help of IRO, 6,500 Mennonite refugees had been moved to Canada, 600 to the United States, and the rest to South America.

The exclusion of German nationals

German nationals had been declared prohibited enemy aliens from September 1939 until September 1950. Since the nationals of most other countries were being readmitted to Canada from 1947 on, German Canadians deeply resented the continued discriminatory exclusion of uprooted Germans

whose friends and relatives wanted to sponsor them in
Canada. A growing lobby including the CCCRR, the Mennonite Central Committee, the German language press in
Canada, and the resurging German-Canadian associations,
such as the Canadian Society for German Relief (in
Kitchener), which was the forerunner of the Trans-Canada
Alliance of German Canadians, as well as several departments
of the federal government, pressured for selective exemptions
from the enemy alien prohibition. As a result, in addition to
the 21,500 *Volksdeutsche*, almost 4,000 natives of Germany
and 5,000 persons of German origin from other countries
were able to enter Canada between 1945 and 1950. The
progressive loosening of the enemy alien restrictions prior to
their complete abolition enabled these Germans to enter
Canada.

At first, the only categories exempted from the prohibition
were children under 18, wives, and proven opponents of the
Nazi regime. In 1947 the Canadian government decided to
recruit a small number of German scientists and technicians
to work in the development of atomic energy and the
establishment of new industries. Starting in 1948 admission
was also loosened for German war brides of Canadian
veterans and residents prior to 1939 of Danzig, when that city
was a Free State. In September 1949 the cabinet decided to
deal favourably with applications from German nationals who
were first-degree relatives (i.e., parents and dependent children) of Canadians. In December 1949 German businessmen
and university students were permitted to enter on visits.
During 1949 government officials also became aware that
ninety per cent of the *Volksdeutsche* who had entered Canada
since 1947 had assumed German citizenship during the Third
Reich. In March 1950, therefore, even those *Volksdeutsche*
and close relatives of Canadians who had accepted German
citizenship after September 1939, were declared admissible.
For all the above mentioned reasons, Canada ended up
admitting some 30,000 persons of German origin before the
last restrictions were removed in September 1950. Thus,
during the period when the admission of German enemy
aliens was officially prohibited, Germans paradoxically ranked
after Poles as Canada's second largest group of non-British
immigrants.

CHAPTER VI

ORIGINS OF THE POST-WORLD WAR II IMMIGRATION

    1. Conditions in occupied Germany
    2. Deportation, expulsion, flight, and resettlement
    3. The Second World War
    4. Stalin and Hitler

Conditions in occupied Germany

Without the large influx of German-speaking immigrants after 1945, the German-Canadian community would be weak and insignificant today. In order to appreciate the adjustment problems of these immigrants, as well as their mentality and aspirations, it is necessary to understand the Old World experiences that uprooted them from their homelands and turned them into emigrants. The Second World War was undoubtedly the most incisive Old World experience shared by the majority of Canada's post-World War II generation of German-speaking immigrants. All Germans in the east and central European countries experienced it and without it most would have had very different futures. The war not only uprooted many of them physically, but also imposed on all of them a new commonality of fate, which detached them from their prewar past and determined their prospects for the future.

The commonality of fate imposed by the Nazi regime on Germans from all over eastern Europe and Germany became manifest in the conditions under which the twelve million surviving German refugees and expellees from the east had to exist in the western zones of occupied Germany for five years. Coming with few or no belongings and frequently unusable skills, they faced enormous difficulties finding adequate housing, food, and jobs among the widespread ruins, shortages, and unemployment. Their intrusion was not welcomed by the suffering local population, and their integration into the local society and disrupted economy appeared impossible. The Allied military government restricted freedom of movement within Germany and forbade emigration from Germany until 1948. Germans could not obtain passports until 1949. In addition, international refugee agencies classified as enemy aliens all ethnic Germans who had sought refuge in Germany during and after the war, and excluded them from all forms of international relief and legal protection available to other displaced persons (see chapter V). The common postwar experience of deprivation, abandonment, and stigmatization forged among Germans of the most divergent backgrounds a new sense of community unique to this generation of immigrants in Canada and elsewhere.

Deportation, expulsion, flight, and resettlement

In 1950 the twelve million German refugees from the east living in West Germany were as numerous as the entire population of Canada. They were categorized according to their manner of displacement from their east European homelands. First, there were the *Volksdeutsche* who had lived in the east European territories conquered by the German Army between 1939 and 1941 and who had fled from the advancing Red Army. These included about 100,000 each from the Soviet Union and Romania, 200,000 from Yugoslavia, and 60,000 from Hungary. For many of them this flight was their second forced migration in less than five years because they had been resettled from South Tyrol, Bessarabia, and the Baltic countries on conquered Polish lands as a result of agreements by Hitler with Mussolini and Stalin in 1939. Second, there were the four million ethnic Germans expelled from Czechoslovakia, Hungary, Romania, and Yugoslavia by these countries' new postwar governments. Third, the annexation of German territory east of the Oder-Neisse line by Poland and the USSR in accordance with the Potsdam Agreement of 1945 led to the expulsion of six million *Reichsdeutsche* from there. Fourth, an estimated 800,000 ethnic Germans were deported to the Soviet Union in 1945 (500,000 civilians to forced labour and 300,000 forcibly repatriated Soviet German refugees). Fewer than one third of these managed to return to the West between 1948 and 1950.

Finally, from the Soviet zone of occupied Germany came a continuous stream of refugees who numbered 1.6 million by 1950. All five categories of displaced Germans were represented among Canada's postwar immigrants.

The Second World War

All the peoples of Europe were profoundly affected by the Second World War. For them it was Nazi Germany's war of conquest, resettlement, and extermination. For Europe's Germans, too, it was a traumatic and tragic experience. Apart from producing a permanent displacement or loss of life of twice as many Germans as the entire population of Canada in 1945, the war has left Germans divided wherever they migrated. Although historical scholarship leaves no doubt that this war was planned and unleashed by Nazi Germany on a confused Europe, most Germans and Austrians experienced it as a war over whose objectives and nature they had little control. Brainwashed into believing that they were serving a worthy cause, they made terrific sacrifices to endure six years of total war at home and on all the fronts. The majority of the ordinary war veterans were preoccupied with staying alive at the front. Some had to witness helplessly and with revulsion the atrocities instigated and committed by special SS task forces against civilian populations in the conquered lands. That generation has found it difficult to accept the postwar judgment that all Germans had to share the guilt for the criminal record of the Nazi regime.

The east European *Volksdeutsche* reacted ambivalently to the German occupation of their homelands and collaborated as much out of necessity as out of choice. Some welcomed the German army as liberators from communist oppression or nationalist discrimination, while some identified with the plight of their non-German host society. Regardless of their attitude, the Third Reich drafted ethnic Germans for German military service and gave them German citizenship. For this they were subsequently punished with permanent expulsion from their centuries-old settlements. Stalin deported the Soviet Germans remaining under his control to Central Asia and Siberia. Many ethnic German families were thus torn literally worlds apart. In the Soviet Union the deportees were accused of treason and disenfranchised for decades, while in the West they were suspected of complicity in war crimes.

Holocaust survivors and victims of Nazi racial policies experienced World War II as an episode of unprecedented crimes against humanity. It was the final act in the Nazi drama of eliminating entire groups of totally innocent Germans as "racially unfit" from the new society envisaged. Under cover of war, millions of German and non-German Jews and their descendants, gypsies, mentally and physically disabled people, political and religious opponents were systematically murdered in prisons or death camps or by specially trained teams. Most of the survivors of this Holocaust found themselves unable to associate again with the perpetrators of these crimes and with the German society that had made the crimes possible.

Hitler and Stalin

The origins and certain unique attitudes of the German post-World War II mass migration to Canada are ultimately traceable to Stalin and Hitler. The impact of both these totalitarian dictators on Europe's German-speaking population is difficult to exaggerate. While Stalin, from the 1930's on, embarked on a policy of systematically destroying the ethnocultural identity of his 1.5 million German-speaking subjects, Hitler's crude perversion of the traditional notion of German ethnicity increasingly shaped his domestic and foreign policies.

The compulsory assimilation of the Soviet Union's national minorities, including the Soviet Germans, into a Russian-speaking classless society was an integral part of Stalin's radical reforms and violent mass purges in the 1930's. Germans under Soviet rule were subjected to collectivization of their farmlands, religious persecution, closure of their schools, churches, and newspapers, and wholesale deportations of able-bodied male members of farming families to forced labour. When Germany invaded the Soviet Union in 1941, Stalin had the innocent German community leaders in the Volga region shot and killed on the pretense that they were Hitler's agents. He banished, with no advance notice and with great loss of life, three quarters of a million Germans from European Russia to various parts of Siberia and Kazakhstan. Mail contacts with Canadian relatives in 1946 revealed their dire fates.

No wonder the non-Russian minorities welcomed Hitler's armies as liberators and collaborated with them, only to be even more severely persecuted after the resurrection of Soviet rule in 1945. On its victorious eastward march, the Red Army took particularly merciless revenge on German communities -- in Romania, Hungary, East Prussia, etc. -- for the cruelties Hitler's rule had inflicted on the Soviet Union. The resulting deep-seated fear of Stalin and hatred of communism was one of the most enduring convictions German refugee immigrants to the New World shared with Baltic and Ukrainian refugees.

Unlike the Baltic and Ukrainian postwar immigrants, however, German immigrants were not proud of their ethnic identity. This was largely the result of the abuse to which Hitler's doctrines and practices had subjected German ethnicity. Hitler viewed *Volk* no longer as a linguistic community whose members shared the same cultural heritage but as a biologically homogeneous super race. *Volkstumsarbeit* and *Deutschtumspflege*, instead of denoting efforts to preserve ethnic identity and cultivate German traditions, came to mean a policy of dehumanizing, expelling, and killing "inferior races" (Jews, Poles, and Ukrainians) and of resettling "Aryan colonists" (Germans from South Tyrol and Russia) on conquered lands. That Hitler was not interested in confining himself to the defense of legitimate ethnocultural interests did not become fully evident until the invasion of Czechoslovakia and Poland. *Volksdeutsche*, who initially had welcomed Hitler's defence of the rights of ethnic minorities, were discredited afterwards as Nazi sympathizers. By 1945 most Germans were shocked to realize that Hitler's regime had perverted every traditional German aspiration and value. After 1945 being German was synonymous with being racist, anti-Semitic, anti-Western, militaristic, and genocidal; consequently the best thing abroad could do was hide their identity.

CHAPTER VII

THE WORLD WAR II EXPERIENCE IN CANADA

1. The impact on ethnocultural life
2. The internment of enemy aliens
3. POW camps
4. Military and alternate service

The impact on ethnocultural life

Historical research has revealed that during World War II the Canadian government did not hold the German people responsible for the policies of the Nazi "gang;" it hence spared German Canadians the severity of maltreatment to which they had been subjected during World War I. Nevertheless, the government was unable to stem the public tide of anti-German sentiment sweeping the country. For the second time within the lifespan of one generation, German ethnicity was singled out as suspect and undesirable in Canada and German Canadians had the experience of being a helpless minority within a hostile society. In the face of this experience the recovery of ethnic confidence after 1945 seemed problematic enough without the postwar discoveries of the atrocities committed by the Nazi regime. These revelations perpetuated the wartime stigmatization of Germans everywhere regardless of their involvement in Nazi war crimes. They also delayed until the 1980's the restoration of respect for German identity and of confidence in its cultivation among all generations of German Canadians.

German-Canadian ethnocultural life was directly affected in three ways by the outbreak of the war. First, all German secular associations suspected of National Socialist or Communist leanings (because of the Hitler-Stalin Pact of August 1939) and of sympathy with the enemy were suppressed and most of their members were arrested and interned. Second, the maintenance of the German language, though not officially prohibited, was severely reduced due to public pressures and widespread apprehensions that their users would identify with the enemy. Third, German-Canadian cultural activities ceased almost completely from fear of provoking resentment and reprisals. German cultural life fell victim to the endeavours among all segments of the German-Canadian community to demonstrate unambiguous loyalty to Canada's war effort. The overall effect of the war was the dissolution of German-Canadian ethnocultural organizations (including many with an outspoken anti-Nazi character), the closure of many German-language schools and newspapers, and the cessation of all noticeable cultural activities associated with Germans.

The internment of enemy aliens

The most drastic and controversial measure which the Canadian government undertook against German Canadians was the arrest and internment of 850 German Canadians. The outbreak of hostilities in September 1939 empowered the government under the War Measures Act (1) to order the registration of all German nationals -- the 1931 census listed 36,000 (22,800 German and 13,000 Austrian citizens) -- and all German-born British subjects in Canada naturalized after September 1929, and (2) to intern, without proof of subversive designs, anyone denounced as being disloyal. By May 1940, 16,600 had registered. In June 1940 the requirement to register as alien enemies and report regularly to the authorities was extended to all those naturalized in Canada after 1922, i.e., some 66,000 German- and Austrian-born Canadians. This was the entire generation of post-World War I German immigrants. Of the 50,000 who registered, about 9,000 remained on parole, while 400 remained interned until 1944 and another 100 until the end of the war.

The names of most of the German Canadians the RCMP arrested in 1939 came from membership lists of German clubs

in such cities as Toronto, Montreal, and Ottawa. Many of
those arrested were ordinary farmers or workers denounced by
other Canadians. The RCMP seized these people -- 303 of
them one week before Canada declared war against Germany
-- without warning, loaded them on trucks and shipped them
to camps in Petawawa, Ontario, and Kananaskis, Alberta.
There they were under prisoner-of-war regulations; their
families were left without any financial support beyond local
relief on the scale provided to the unemployed. Review
tribunals hearing the appeals of the internees produced clear
evidence that most of even those accused of membership in
pro-Nazi organizations had done so for reasons that had little
to do with politics or ideology. Rather, they were unemployed
new immigrants interested in the material fringe benefits, such
as free health and unemployment insurance, that these
organizations had offered.

The parolees and internees were thus the victims of an
unfounded Nazi scare in Canada and of the government's
desire to demonstrate to the public that it had successfully
squashed a "Fifth Column" conspiracy, i.e., the enemy within
the country. German Canadians had given as little cause for
their punitive treatment as had Japanese Canadians, and the
internment of the former served as a model for the treatment
of the latter. Yet, unlike Japanese Canadians, German
Canadians have never asked for nor been offered an apology
or financial compensation by Canada.

POW camps

During World War II, 35,000 German soldiers captured in
the battlefields of Europe and North Africa and on the high
seas were put behind barbed wire in Canada. They spent the
rest of the war in the 26 major detention camps set up in
Quebec, Ontario, and Alberta and in hosts of smaller work
camps. The German POWs had to share some of these camps
with interned Canadian enemy aliens, with pro-Nazis and
Communists, with the crews from seized enemy merchant
vessels, and with 2,500, mostly Jewish, refugee internees sent
from Britain in 1940. There were conflicts and fights between
pro-Nazis and anti-Nazis and between Nazi POWs and

German Jewish refugee internees. The Canadian authorities, unaware of the ideological dimensions of this war and its impact on life in the POW camps, were slow in sorting out the problems. The antagonistic groups were shuttled to different camps and most of the anti-Nazi inmates and refugees were released in small batches between 1941 and 1943.

All reports on the POWs indicate they were treated relatively well. They were paid for their work and given considerable freedom. Some married Canadians and many liked Canada so well they did not want to return to Germany in 1945. However, German POWs were initially not welcomed in Canada. The war propaganda had brainwashed Canadians to hate and fear Germans. By 1944 most POWs had been moved to logging camps, farms, and construction sites. Canadians not only came to rely on their labour as indispensable to the war economy, they were impressed with the POWs' willingness to engage in the kind of hard physical work most Canadians declined. In 1946 a lobby of farmers, logging companies, and manufacturers pleaded in vain with the government to give some of the POWs the choice of staying in Canada even though international law required that all be returned to Germany. When German nationals were readmitted to Canada in 1950, numerous former POWs were among the new influx of immigrants.

Military and alternate service

German Canadians responded to the Canadian government's call to arms against the united German-Austrian Reich without any noticeable reservations. In mid-1943 even those declared to be enemy aliens were paradoxically allowed to enlist, provided they applied for naturalization. In 1944, when the government introduced conscription for overseas service, German immigrant families who had been classified as enemy aliens, refused naturalization, and, in some cases, interned and denaturalized, watched helplessly while their sons were drafted. By late 1944, an estimated 36,000 German-speaking Canadians were in the Canadian armed forces.

Canada's traditionally pacifist Mennonites bitterly debated

what kind of -- if any -- alternative to military service they should undertake. In the 1920's Mennonites, like other immigrants, had been admitted to Canada with the understanding that neither they nor their children would be exempted from any laws applicable to Canadian citizens in general. Furthermore, public opinion was also an important factor. Many Mennonites were considered to have already compromised their religious principles by adopting modern ways. Public opinion opposed conscientious objection to all forms of government service -- the policy in World War I -- because it seemed to be a scheme whereby the Mennonites could supposedly fill their pockets at home while other Canadians were serving their country. Thus, during World War II Mennonites who claimed CO status were required to provide one of three alternative services (1) in work camps set up in National Parks or at Forest Experimental Stations, (2) in agriculture or industry, or (3) in the Royal Canadian Army Medical Corps and the Canadian Dental Corps as medics. In fact, 63 percent of Canada's total number of 11,000 conscientious objectors were Mennonites. Nevertheless, an equal number of Canadian Mennonites are estimated to have entered combatant service and some *Russländer* Mennonites were reported as serving with distinction in the battlefields of Europe.

CHAPTER VIII

BETWEEN THE WORLD WARS

1. Cultural and club life
2. The impact of National Socialism
3. Economic hardships and contributions
4. Canadianization and generational conflict

Cultural and club life

On the eve of the Second World War, German-Canadian cultural activities presented the image of a vibrant and self-confident community. Not only did German Canadians appear to have recovered from the devastating blows dealt by World War I dealt to their image and cultural life, but between the world wars their ethnocultural aspirations found forms of expression and embarked on directions different from those of earlier times. What was new, above all, was the emergence of a group consciousness among German Canadians of different generations, denominations, and geographic backgrounds. Distinct ethnocultural aspirations manifested themselves on the local, regional, and national levels in a number of ways. Notable activities ranged from the celebration of *Deutsche Tage* to the first serious endeavours to record the group's history and contributions. The variety of secular clubs and associations that sprouted in the 1920's and 1930's was unprecedented.

The revitalization of German-Canadian cultural life after World War I took a full decade and was closely linked to the reopening of Canada to German immigration from central and eastern Europe. This new generation of immigrants was moulded by two important experiences: Germany's and

Austria's national humiliation and the arising discrimination against German-speaking minorities in the newly formed national states of eastern Europe. The strong German ethnic consciousness of these immigrants was the driving force behind the slowly surging demand for restitution of Canada's German-language culture, a self-evident right before 1914. The editors of Canada's revived German-language newspapers, such as Bernhard Bott who was *Der Courier's* editor from 1923 to 1934, and the organizers of local clubs and regional ethnic associations led the campaign for the public recognition of German Canadians' historic rights.

In 1928, prewar and postwar immigrants in Manitoba and Alberta successfully launched the celebrations of *Deutsche Tage* -- annual ethnic reunions, initially organized as picnics, with speeches, folkdances, singing, and cultural exhibitions. By 1934 these had spread from Edmonton and Winnipeg to Vancouver, Regina, and Kitchener. Their intent was to overcome the divisions among German Canadians and to rally them behind common symbols and values. During these years Bott collected information from surviving pioneers in western Canada; historian Heinz Lehmann later used these recollections as a basis for the first comprehensive historical account of German Canadians. A growing network of voluntary German language schools and cultural competitions and festivals, organized by German clubs and associations, sought to maintain and entrench the German heritage in Canada.

Local German language clubs and regional associations, prohibited during World War I, did not reappear in Canada until the mid- and late 1920's. With few exceptions, such as the *Volksverein deutsch-kanadischer Katholiken* (founded 1909 in Winnipeg), prewar secular organizations were not revived. Instead, the proliferating club life of the 1920's and 1930's mirrored the origins, lifestyles, and aspirations of the postwar immigrants. The large urban centers now had more German clubs than ever before, and many of them were run for the first time by and for *Volksdeutsche.* In the early 1930's many local clubs attached themselves to provincial and regional umbrella organizations, such as the *Deutsch-Kanadisches Zentralkomitee,* the *Deutsche Arbeitsgemeinschaft,* and the *Deutsch-Kanadische Bund von Manitoba.* Simultaneously, new secular associations on the regional and national levels with local affiliates, such as the *Deutsch-Kanadische Verband von Saskatchewan* and the *Deutscher Bund Canada*, advocated the diverse denominational, ideological, political, or cultural interests of German Canadians. The proliferation of associations reflected the strong consciousness of German identity shared by *Reichsdeutsche*, *Volksdeutsche*, Austrians, and Mennonite newcomers alike and rooted in their common experience of having suffered as "Germans" during and after the First World War.

The impact of National Socialism

Adolf Hitler's assumption of power in Germany was accompanied by the widespread anticipation of a better future for Germany and Germans everywhere. Not only was Hitler given credit for the restoration of Germany's economy, domestic order, and national honour, but his regime claimed to care for the welfare of Germans everywhere. Germans everywhere, Nazi propaganda proclaimed, formed a world-wide German *Volksgemeinschaft*, to which they owed as much allegiance as to the country where they resided. That this appeal to the *Volksgemeinschaft* struck a responsive chord among the *Volksdeutsche* in Europe is not surprising and can easily be misinterpreted. Since they lived in a non-German environment and had never been part of a modern German nation state, they could relate to their ethnic identity only as members of a wider German ethnic community, or *Volk*, that shared a common language, culture, and descent. The discrimination against the *Volksdeutsche* in the newborn nation states of postwar eastern Europe had caused a desire among them for closer identification with the wider German community. They were searching for help, orientation, and inspiration from Germany, even before Hitler's takeover.

The international atmosphere of grudging respect, if not admiration, for Adolf Hitler's Germany of the mid-1930's was, no doubt, conducive to a resurgence of pride in Canada in the German cultural heritage. German Canadians, it must be kept in mind, were in no better position to perceive the true totalitarian objectives of the Nazi regime than the British prime ministers Lloyd George, Neville Chamberlain, and even Winston Churchill, who admired Hitler and trusted his motives until March 1939. In Canada, Prime Minister William Lyon Mackenzie King was so impressed with the great "constructive" work Hitler had achieved in Germany that in February 1939 he still assured Hitler of his "friendship," and as late as July 1939 accepted a personal invitation from Hitler to be among a group of Canadians to visit Germany for three weeks. German war preparations (un)fortunately interfered with the travel arrangements.

Hitler's rise to power boosted the ethnic self-confidence of many German Canadians -- noticeable in the 1936 Census returns where a higher proportion of Canadians reported their origin as German -- and brought to a head the budding of the first German-Canadian group consciousness among Mennonite, *volksdeutsche*, and *reichsdeutsche* circles. Nevertheless, attempts to organize German Canadians in the service of the Nazi cause failed. The *Deutscher Bund Canada*, founded in 1934 to promote the ideals of the new Germany, had the largest membership (about 2,000, mostly in western Canada) of the pro-Nazi organizations. Ironically, its popularity may be attributable partly to its leaders' claim that the *Bund's* goals were cultural and not political and that its members had to be honourable and law-abiding residents of Canada. Its official organ was the *Deutsche Zeitung für Canada* with 5,000 subscribers. The *NSDAP* (Nazi Party) itself had no more than 170 members in Canada, and its affiliated *Deutsche Arbeitsfront (DAF)* an estimated 500. On the other hand, the membership of anti-Nazi German-Canadian organizations, such as the German-Canadian League (since 1934), the pro-Communist *Deutscher Arbeiter und Farmerverband* (since 1933), and the *St. Peters Bote*, was equally high or even higher. It is true that Nazi organizers tried to promote the union of a region's German clubs into manipulable *Arbeitsgemeinschaften* and succeeded after 1936 in exploiting the annual *Deutsche Tage* for their purposes. Compared with the documented manifestations of fascism and anti-Semitism among French Canadians and English Canadians in the 1930's, however, the direct influence of National Socialism on German Canadians appears to have been negligible.

Economic hardships and contributions

The pro-Nazi and pro-Communist lobbies organized by German Canadians were two extremes among a variety of Canadian fringe groups spawned by the Great Depression of 1930-1940. These offered not only a radical cure (namely, the models of Soviet Russia or Nazi Germany) for the grave economic and social ills afflicting Canada in the 1930's, but also mutual aid and subsistence to many recent immigrants who were unable to gain a foothold. Newcomers, especially those of non-British origin, were even more severely affected by the Depression than the rest of the population. Many lost their newly acquired farms because they could not repay their mortgages, and even more of them had to bury their plans to become farmers. For the few jobs available, immigrants -- and German-speaking ones were no exception -- were among the last to be hired, and public pressure saw to it that "hyphenated" Canadians were among the first ones to be fired. Sometimes it is difficult for Canadians today to understand the hardship of unemployment in the 1930's. People in those days did not have the buffer of unemployment compensation or any government social security scheme to support them. Prior to the Depression, male immigrants used to arrive in Canada ahead of their families in order to establish an economic base for the rest of the family to follow. But the effects of the Depression and the war caused many immigrants to remain separated from their families until after the war or forever.

German Canadians were not only victims of economic changes in the 1920's and 1930's; they also made significant contributions to the economy. Rapid industrial growth in the 1920's caused an exodus of Canadians from the rural to the urban areas and created a rural demand for immigrant farmers and farm labour. Farming thus remained a viable sector of the Canadian economy, in part because recent as well as established German Canadians accepted a way of life increasingly shunned by native British Canadians. Unwanted in urban occupations and discriminated against on the job market, Mennonite and other ethnic German settlers made a virtue of necessity and successfully pioneered agricultural development and promoted cooperative enterprise. In the

so-called Chicken and Garden Village of North Kildonan near
Winnipeg, Mennonites initiated large-scale urbanizing agriculture and in Coaldale (Alberta), profitable sugar-beet farming.
They expanded the orchards of the Pacific coast, southern
Ontario, and Nova Scotia. The establishment of the Reesor
settlement in the impenetrable bush of northern Ontario was
hailed as one of the most difficult pioneering accomplishments of immigrants anywhere in Canada.

German Canadians took up the challenges of the northern
wilderness, the bush land of Saskatchewan, and the dry land of
Alberta. On the Peace River, Hermann Trelle, known as the
"wheat king," demonstrated the profitability of wheat growing
and attracted a stream of settlers to the far north of Alberta
after 1926. German immigrants engaged successfully in
dairying, truck gardening, and wheat growing. The proverbial
agricultural genius of German farmers in general, and of
Mennonites in particular, was proven during the difficult years
of the 1930's, when well-established German wheat producers
in the prairies were spared economic ruin by switching to
mixed farming.

Canadianization and generational conflict

The fervently pro-British and anti-foreign sentiments stirred
up by World War I propaganda continued to be a dominant
force through the 1920's under the label of Canadianization
and posed a serious threat to the survival of a German
ethnocultural identity in Canada. Canadianization stood for
the renunciation by non-British immigrants of their ancestral
culture in favor of the behavior and values of the British
group. The main vehicle for the promotion of Canadianization
was compulsory attendance at the English-language public
school by the children of all non-English-speaking Canadians.
This was enacted into law throughout English Canada during
World War I. The Canadianization campaign was radicalized
by nativists, veterans' organizations, and labour leaders who
pointed hysterically to the revelation of the 1921 census that
41 percent of the population of the prairie provinces claimed
non-British origin. The nativists whipped up apprehensions
that Canada's cultural diversity and foreign immigration

would destroy Canadian laws and institutions. In post-World War I Canada the assimilation of the "foreigner" thus became a priority of the first order. Canada's policy of multiculturalism, proclaimed in 1971, constituted a break with this past.

These pressures to conform made life difficult for newcomers who by their very nature were unable to assimilate immediately. Religious minorities who considered the German language a part of their religious heritage were under particular stress. At the same time, these pressures accelerated the assimilation of later-generation German Canadians who, in their struggle for material survival and upward social mobility, wanted to overcome the stigma of their non-British background. The Canadianization drive of the 1920's thus widened the generation gap between the prewar immigrants and their Canadian-born children on the one hand and between both of these and the postwar newcomers on the other hand. It divided the Mennonite community into those who accepted the English-language public school without strong reservations, those who decided to resist this worldly intrusion as much as possible, and a minority who found these pressures so unacceptable that they emigrated to Latin America.

CHAPTER IX

REFUGEES FROM THE THIRD REICH

1. The Depression and refugee immigration to Canada
2. The exclusion of German Jews
3. The admission of Sudeten Germans
4. The transfer of internees from Britain

The Depression and refugee immigration to Canada

Refugees, it has been argued, always arrive at the wrong time, never at a convenient time. This was particularly true for those who were deprived of their civil rights and fearing for their lives under Hitler's dictatorship in the 1930's when they sought a haven in Canada. Large numbers of German-speaking refugees came not only from Germany but also from the countries annexed or threatened with occupation by Nazi Germany prior to the outbreak of World War II and from those whose governments were closely allied with Hitler. An estimated 450,000 German-speaking people fled Europe in the 1930's because of racial, religious, political, or intellectual persecution. Of those, Canada accepted fewer than 4,000 and Newfoundland, at that time not yet a part of Canada, only 12.

In Canada and Newfoundland these refugees were unwanted for a number of reasons. First, with the onset of the Depression and Canadians' and Newfoundlanders' intense preoccupation with their own economic problems, the governments banned all non-agricultural immigrants, unless they were British or American. Only those with enough capital for starting and operating a viable farm were eligible for admission. In practice, however, the governments of the Prairie provinces rejected all schemes to settle European farmers who pursued a culturally dissimilar way of life.

Second, anti-foreign sentiments, which had never fully subsided in the 1920's, rose sharply as Canadians saw their accustomed lifestyle and standard of living endangered. The central European refugee was viewed as an alien who brought foreign ideas, such as communism, fascism, and nazism. Jewish and Asian refugees were considered objectionable on racial grounds. Third, since many of the refugees of the 1930's were highly trained specialists, there was great concern that their expertise and skills might cost Canadians jobs. Organized labour and professional associations, therefore, joined hands in opposing refugee immigration. The humanitarian needs of the refugees were considered secondary. The attitude of the public and the government was one of indifference, if not hostility, to the plight of the refugee.

The exclusion of German Jews

Most of the German-speaking refugees in the 1930's were those classified as Jewish (i.e., anyone having one Jewish grandparent, regardless of whether the person still adhered to the Jewish faith) by the Nazi regime. They included therefore many who considered themselves as German as any other ethnic German. Perhaps their parents or grandparents had abandoned the Jewish faith or they had lived in German areas for a long time. Their step-by-step exclusion from public, professional, and social life in Germany began with Hitler's takeover in January 1933 and turned into a campaign of violent persecution in 1938, especially in the newly annexed areas of Austria, Czechoslovakia, and Danzig. Compared with the exodus of 150,000 refugees from Nazi Germany between 1933 and September 1938, more than twice as many people fled the enlarged Third Reich in the following year.

In the late 1930's tens of thousands of German Jewish refugees petitioned, appealed, and pleaded for admission to Canada. Statistical data indicate that from 1931 to 1938 Canada admitted no more than 79 Jews born in Germany and 39 born in Austria. Instead of dealing with the acute refugee problem in a manner commensurate with its resources, international role, and commitments, in 1938 Canada restricted Jewish refugee immigration even more. Britain, half of whose 65,000 refugees from the Third Reich were Austrian Jews, was unable to persuade its Commonwealth partner Canada to admit more than 82 of those Jews between 1939 and 1941. The immigration difficulties of the renowned physicist Gerhard Herzberg, later proudly acclaimed as Canada's first Nobel Prize winner, reveal that even a preeminent German scientist was suspect and unwelcome, especially because his spouse was Jewish. Nothing illustrates Canada's policy of virtually excluding Jewish refugees better than the government's refusal in June 1939 to allow the landing of the luxury liner *St. Louis*. It had 905 German Jews aboard who had fled from Hamburg in search of a safe haven. After having been turned away from Latin-American countries and the United States, as well as from Canada, the *St. Louis* was forced to return to Europe where many of the refugees were killed.

Anti-Semitism was pervasive and widespread in French- and English-speaking Canada in the 1930's and 1940's. Historical research has revealed that Canada's Director of Immigration from 1936 to 1943, Frederick Charles Blair, was an anti-Semite and that his Department applied unabashedly racial and anti-Semitic criteria in the selection of immigrants and refugees until three years after some of the death camps had been liberated. Pointing to Canada's record as the worst among all possible refugee-receiving countries in the 1930's, historians have concluded that Canada must share some responsibility for the fate of the Jews in the Third Reich.

The admission of Sudeten Germans

In striking contrast to the indiscriminate exclusion of German Jewish refugees from Canada was the scheme for settling 1,200 families of Sudeten German refugees in western Canada in 1939. The credit for the initiation and partial realization of this scheme belongs entirely to the British government. Britain was one of the main parties to the Munich Agreement of September 1938, by which Czechoslovakia was divided and its western part, the Sudetenland, with its three million German-speaking Czech citizens was handed over to Hitler's Germany. The British were, therefore, also prepared to assume some responsibility for the refugee problem caused by the Munich Agreement and arranged a ten million pound loan for the resettlement of 20,000 Czech- and 10,000 German-speaking refugees who had fled from the Sudetenland and were living in temporary camps near Prague.

In response to British pressures, the Canadian government agreed to accept up to 1,200 physically fit German-speaking families from this group of refugees for settlement on railway land, provided the British government would finance the resettlement with a $1,500 grant per family. The unanimous opposition of the four western Canadian premiers to the block settlement desired by these Social Democratic Sudeten Germans and the search for a suitable site delayed the evacuation of the refugees from Prague until it was too late. Most of the designated families were trapped by the German occupation of Prague in March 1939 and barred from emigrating. Of the 300 families and individuals who had managed to reach the safety of England, 148 families (525 individuals) were sent to abandoned farms on Canadian National Railway lands near St. Walberg in northeastern Saskatchewan, while 152 families (518 individuals) were settled in the wilderness of Tupper Creek (now Tomslake) in northeastern British Columbia. These 1,043 Sudeten Germans were the first and only substantial group of Europe's pre-World War II refugees permitted to enter Canada.

The Sudeten settlers experienced many difficulties in their often hastily improvised arrangements at the frontier of North American civilization. As highly urbanized and skilled industrial workers from one of Europe's manufacturing centres, they had to overcome almost insurmountable hurdles in their attempt to adapt to homesteading in this no-man's land. About one third of the settlers migrated to central Canada where the labour shortage during World War II enabled them to assume industrial employment. In Hamilton they founded the Sudeten Club in November 1941, at a time when most other German clubs had been dissolved. After the war they initiated aid and immigration programs for thousands of the six million Sudeten Germans expelled by the postwar Czech governments. The Sudeten German Social Democratic settlers of 1939 have assiduously endeavoured to maintain their separate ideological and cultural identity, not only within the German-Canadian ethnic mosaic, but also vis-à-vis non-Social Democratic Sudeten German refugees who immigrated to Canada after the Second World War.

The transfer of internees from Britain

The only other party of German-speaking refugees from the pre-World War II period consisted of was the so-called "accidental immigrants" who were more or less deported to Canada. These consisted of 2,300 males of the 65,000 (mostly Jewish) refugees from Germany residing in Britain. The 2,300 had been interned in Britain in the spring of 1940 after the German occupation of France, Belgium, and the Netherlands seemed to make a German invasion of the British Isles imminent. They were sent to Canada under false pretenses and without the full consent of the Canadian government. The Canadian government had agreed to a temporary transfer of 4,000 enemy alien civilians and 3,000 POWs, but not of any refugees. Since the British, however, held no more than 4,500 men in the agreed-upon categories, they made up the difference with refugee internees. The internees were transported with the others in three prison ships, one of which was sunk by a German submarine resulting in heavy loss of life.

In Canada the refugees were received as dangerous enemy aliens and detained in internment camps with pro-Nazi prisoners and internees. The latter organized anti-Semitic demonstrations and acts of vandalism against the Jewish refugees. It took the Canadian authorities months to realize that they had mistakenly imprisoned homeless refugees. The refugees were then transferred to different camps in Quebec and New Brunswick. The first ones were released in February 1941, but some inexplicably remained interned until August 1943. Of these refugee internees, 972 stayed in Canada. Most of the others returned to England. Among those who stayed were geophysicist Ernst Deutsch, urbanist Peter Oberländer, theologian Gregory Baum, musicologist Helmut Kalmann, mathematician Walter Kohn, philosopher Emil Fackenheim, writers Carl Weiselberger, Henry Kreisel, Eric Koch, Charles Wassermann and Franz Kramer, lyricist Anton Frisch, artist

Oscar Cahen, architect Henry Fliess, pianist John Newmark, and art promoters Max Stern and Walter Homburger. The significant contributions to Canada these and many others of the refugee internees have made as scientists, academicians, artists, musicians, and writers indicate what invaluable talents Canada spurned by closing its doors to more refugees from the Third Reich.

CHAPTER X

IMMIGRATION FROM GERMANY BETWEEN THE
WORLD WARS

1. Canadian immigration policy
2. The push factors
3. The role of the railways and churches
4. The structure of the migration

Canadian immigration policy

Between the two world wars more than 100,000 German-speaking Europeans immigrated to Canada. Migration statistics indicate that one quarter of these were *Reichsdeutsche* and that most of them came between 1927 and 1930. Canadian census data, however, reveal that less than two thirds of these *Reichsdeutsche* immigrants remained in Canada and that the remainder moved on to the United States. The reasons for the large immigration from Germany for a period of no more than four years and the movement of such a high percentage of these immigrants to the United States must be sought in Canadian and American immigration policies.

After World War I both countries pursued immigration policies that restricted immigration according to the desirability of the immigrants' national and ethnic origins. America allowed persons born in Germany a quota of 25,814 per year while Canadians were outside the American quota system. Canada distinguished between "most preferred" immigrants (British and American), "preferred" (French, Belgian, Dutch, Swiss, and Scandinavian), "non-preferred" (the remaining European countries), and "prohibited" (most Asians) categories.

Until 1923 Canada prohibited immigration from Germany. Thereafter Germans were classified among the non-preferred category, but in 1926 they were promoted to the "preferred" category. Prior to 1931 Canada wanted agriculturists to occupy and cultivate marginal land in the West. To this end it recruited farmers, agricultural labourers, and domestic servants from the non-preferred countries. Immigrants with non-agricultural occupations were admitted only from the preferred countries. Because of American quota restrictions, Canada became the choice of many Germans who preferred to migrate to America. In Canada, German immigrants became eligible for admission to the United States after a one- or two-year residence. Between 1927 and 1930 Canada, after the United States, thus became the most preferred destination for emigrants from Germany. In 1931, due to the Depression, Canada restricted immigration to British and Americans, wealthy farmers, and close relatives of Canadians.

The push factors

Germany's defeat in the First World War and its disastrous consequences caused a widespread desire among Germans to emigrate. The influx of 1.4 million refugees, mostly from the territories lost by the Treaty of Versailles, and the reduction of Germany by 13 percent of its prewar territory, increased population density at a time when millions of Germans had become economically and socially uprooted. Revolutionary upheavals, civil war, unemployment, inflation, and the severe devaluation of the German currency between 1919 and 1924 made many Germans lose faith in the future of their country. The sense of social and economic insecurity was pervasive even during the period of Germany's economic and political stabilization from 1924 to 1929. Apprehensions were fuelled by the propaganda of the Communist, Conservative, and right radical parties, which continued to question the Weimar Republic's foundations and prospects. Fear of the future and of unemployment coupled with social decline plus the yearning to become self-reliant on one's own farm became powerful motives for emigration among urban Germans in the 1920's. The opportunities Canada offered to farmers appealed to these Germans. At the same time, a chronic agricultural crisis in southwestern and northeastern Germany led to a continuous migration from rural to urban areas. A better future in Canada than the uncertain employment prospects in German industry seemed to beckon many small farmers and agricultural labourers from these regions.

The sudden surge in unemployment in Germany with the onset of the Great Depression, accompanied by the specter of escalating political violence between Nazis and Communists, was reflected in a corresponding urge to emigrate, which was duly registered by the official emigrant information offices. Nevertheless, it did not translate into a significantly higher volume of emigration in 1929 and 1930 because the unemployed lacked the money to emigrate. Then in March 1931 Canada virtually closed its gates to German immigrants. After Hitler's takeover in 1933, emigration from Germany, except for refugee movements, ceased and a return migration from Canada to Germany started. While the Depression continued to rage unabatedly in Canada, Nazi Germany was admired for undertaking seemingly successful measures to restore employment and political stability.

The role of the railways and churches

The Canadian government put the immigration and settlement of "agriculturists, agricultural workers, and domestic servants" from the non-preferred countries (which included most of the German-speaking immigrants in the period between the wars) in the hands of the two Canadian railway companies, the Canadian Pacific Railway (CPR) and the Canadian National Railway (CNR). These were most interested in recruiting immigrants for settling their vacant lands, and for the purpose of organizing every aspect of the settlement process they formed the Canada Colonization Association, a CPR subsidiary, with the German American T.O.F. Herzer as manager. In Canada, the CNR and CPR sought contact with existing ethnic settlements to encourage them to induce the emigration of friends and relatives from Europe. Systematic cooperation of the railways with the churches of the prospective settlers was achieved through the establishment of Mennonite, Baptist, Lutheran, and Catholic immigration boards. Their role was to assist in settler recruitment and selection of the newcomers' district and employment.

The Canadian church boards coordinated their activities with the emigrant information and aid organizations of their denominational counterparts in Germany. German church organizations undertook the selection and preparation of the emigrants in Germany. Often in collaboration with the steamship agencies commissioned by the Canadian railways, these church organizations arranged in the emigrants' parish in Germany for passage, housing, and jobs at the Canadian destination. Upon arrival in Canada the immigrants were transferred to the care of their railway and church boards, which provided the last link in this "chain service" by guiding the immigrants to their prospective employers and parishes. Among receiving countries, Canada was unique in arranging such a comprehensive system of guidance for migrants from their place of origin in Germany to final their destination. That this was a major factor facilitating German migration to Canada in the late 1920's is undeniable.

The structure of the migration

The significance of the "chain service" arranged by the Canadian railways and churches is reflected in the fact that from 1927 to 1930, 67 percent of the Canadian immigrants from Germany were farm labourers, mostly from the agrarian regions of northeastern Germany. This percentage is three times higher than the percentage of farm labourers among the total emigration from Germany (to all countries) during 1927-1930. The percentage of domestic servants among Germans immigrating to Canada during the period 1922-1931 (10 percent) was approximately the same as that for the total German emigration for this period (12 percent). The 3.4 percent Germans who were skilled workers among those immigrating to Canada during 1922-1931, however, is far below the total number of craftsmen and skilled workers emigrating from Germany (31 percent) during this period.

An examination of the social structure of the German immigration to Canada 1922-1931 reveals that exactly half the

immigrants were men, and one quarter each were women and
children. While nearly half the total number of emigrants
from Germany in 1929 were between 20 and 40 years old,
nearly three quarters of the Germans emigrating to Canada
between 1922 and 1931 were in that age group. Germany's
typical emigrant to Canada in the late 1920's was a 26-
year-old, single farmer.

CHAPTER XI

IMMIGRATION FROM CENTRAL AND EASTERN EUROPE

1. The cultural role of the ethnic Germans
2. The ethnic German emigration from eastern Europe
3. The rescue of the *Russländer*
4. *Russländer* and *Kanadier* Mennonites

The cultural role of the ethnic Germans

Around sixty percent of Canada's 100,000 German immigrants between the world wars were ethnic Germans from eastern European countries. They came from the Soviet Union (30,000), Romania and Yugoslavia (14,000), Poland (8,000), Austria (5,000), Czechoslovakia (3,000), and Hungary (2,000). In Canada their cultural role has been significant in three respects. First, it may be argued that without them Canada's German-language culture - crippled and subdued as a result of World War I and the postwar drive for Canadianization - would probably have been doomed. These ethnic Germans not only shaped the culture of the postwar German-Canadian community, but also encouraged the intimidated prewar generations to retain their cultural heritage.

Second, the infusion of some 60,000 ethnic Germans (in comparison with merely 20,000 natives of Germany) confirmed the pre-World War I composition of the German-Canadian community in contrast to the German-American community, in which the *Reichsdeutsche* were dominant. The culture of the ethnic German immigrants, in accordance with their east European background, was rural and church-oriented. This culture epitomized the often parochial preservation of old

German traditions and folkways that had already disappeared in 20th-century urban Germany. However, the experience of being stigmatized and persecuted as "Germans" by their host societies during and after World War I reinforced in these Germans a consciousness of their ethnicity and caused many of them to identify with the wider German community in cultural activities, secular associations, and socio-political aspirations. Third, the 60,000 ethnic German immigrants of the 1920's were instrumental in opening Canada's gates to *volksdeutsche* refugees and expellees after the end of World War II. As first-degree family sponsors and through their church organizations, they were able to organize the admission of nearly 30,000 ethnic German refugees between 1947 and 1950, when Canada prohibited the entry of "German enemy aliens."

Particularly important in these respects were the 21,000 Mennonite immigrants from the Soviet Union. Among the postwar influx of ethnic Germans they formed the largest and most homogeneous group. Due to their relatively high levels of education and urbanization -- they included many middle class professionals, such as teachers, writers, physicians, estate owners, bankers, businessmen, and clerks -- and their desire to identify with the wider German-Canadian community, they were predestined to play a leading cultural role in that community from the 1930's to the 1960's. Because of their own tumultuous historical experiences from 1914 to 1921, they searched for orientation and inspiration from Germany in the 1930's and undertook great sacrifices to rescue Mennonite refugees from the ravages of World War II. Labelled *Russländer* by the long-established Canadian Mennonites, they can be credited with making outstanding contributions to secular German literature in Canada, defending the cultural interests of the German-Canadian community, and maintaining their distinct identity within the Mennonite community.

The ethnic German emigration from eastern Europe

Conditions in the native countries of the ethnic Germans after the First World War provided a variety of reasons for their desire to emigrate to Canada. The homelands of some of them, especially those from Volhynia (now part of Poland), had been theatres of war and their settlements had suffered terribly. Members of privileged minorities in the Habsburg and Romanov empire before the war, most ethnic Germans suffered political discrimination in the newly created postwar national states. Some centuries-old areas of German settlement were divided among three countries without regard to ethnic or economic ties. The Banat, for example, became parts of Yugoslavia, Romania, and Hungary. Large German-speaking regions like the Sudetenland and German Austria were deprived of their former markets and of the right to self-determination. The persecution of religion and wealth in Russia during the Communist revolution and the ensuing civil war dealt a particularly destructive blow to the once prosperous German farming communities in the Ukraine and ethnic German estates in the Baltic and was responsible for an unprecedented mass flight of Germans.

There were two reasons why many ethnic German refugees migrated to Canada instead of to another country in the Americas. The American immigration quota system, unveiled in 1921, allotted quotas based on citizenship rather than on ethnic identity, and only a minimal quota was granted to citizens of east European countries. Accordingly, the American national quota law severely limited the immigration of Germans from Russia to the United States because it classified them as east Europeans. Second, the refugees preferred Canada to such Latin American countries as Mexico due primarily to Canada's political and legal stability. Moreover, relatives of the ethnic Germans who had immigrated to Canada before the war, as well as German-Canadian churches and relief organizations, provided a supportive network by sponsoring and facilitating the immigration to Canada, once the legal barriers had been removed.

The rescue of the *Russländer* Mennonites

In the upheavals that led to the establishment of the Communist regime, Russia's 120,000 prosperous German-speaking Mennonites suffered a particularly harsh fate because of their religion, wealth, and conscientious objection.

Helplessly exposed during the Civil War of 1918-1920 to indiscriminate torture, murder, and plunder, they suspended their principle of nonresistance and formed Home Defence units *(Selbstschutz)*. The victorious Communist regime in turn disenfranchised and expropriated them as counter-revolutionaries and enemies of the Soviet state. In order to overcome their stigma and achieve permission to emigrate, they organized the Union of Citizens of Dutch Ancestry in 1922. For Canada's established post-World War I community of 50,000 Mennonites the problems of organizing, financing, and settling tens of thousands of their coreligionists from Soviet Russia were formidable. No precedent existed in the history of Mennonite migrations for an organized group movement on a similar scale.

The first step was undertaken by American Mennonites with the foundation of the Mennonite Central Committee (MCC) in 1920. Its initial purpose was to coordinate relief action to ensure the physical survival of the Russian Mennonites during the famine of 1920-22. In its search for a suitable place of resettlement for 100,000 Russian Mennonites, MCC decided in favor of Canada for three reasons. In 1921 America introduced its immigration quota system thereby reducing east European immigration to a trickle, while Canada's newly elected Liberal government of W.L. Mackenzie King rescinded Canada's three-year ban on Mennonite immigration. In Canada, furthermore, the two national railways (CPR and CNR) had had excellent experiences with the pre-World War I settlement of Russian Mennonites in the prairies and offered land and loans along with special passage rates from Communist Russia to western Canada as incentives to attract more Mennonite settlers from Russia.

To arrange the sale of railway land and the repayment of the travel debt *(Reiseschuld)* to the railways, Canadian Mennonites formed the Canadian Mennonite Board of Colonization (CMBC) in 1922. (Both MCC and CMBC played a major role again in the post-World War II rescue of Mennonite refugees.) The migration of the 21,000 *Russländer* to Canada took place in small installments between 1923 and 1932 and under the greatest difficulties. Whereas the Soviet government refused to allow large numbers of Mennonites to emigrate, the Canadian government restricted immigration by a petty enforcement of health regulations. It became necessary to establish transit camps in Germany and England for the hundreds of Mennonites who were allowed neither to enter Canada nor to return to Soviet Russia. The migration came to an end between 1929 and 1932 when Stalin stopped all further emigration in connection with his new economic policies, and Canada closed its gates to European immigrants because of the Depression.

Russländer and *Kanadier* Mennonites

The distinct identity acquired by the *Russländer* as a result of the experiences preceding their emigration set them apart from the earlier generations of German Mennonites from Russia who had come to western Canada between 1874 and 1914. The latter were now labelled *Kanadier* and distinguished from the *Russländer*, and both of these contrasted with the Ontario Swiss Mennonites who arrived in the 1780's (see chapter XXIV). These three groupings have remained three of the main cultural divisions among Canadian Mennonites. To the *Russländer*, the *Kanadier* seemed too unwilling to interact with the real world around them and too fixated on rigid adherence to tradition, whether in liturgy, social customs, the use of Low instead of High German, or in their fear of schools and education. Considering the centuries-long separate development, the *Russländers'* communication gap with the Swiss Mennonites was understandably great. The *Russländer* found it impossible to adapt to the Swiss conservatism, excessively simple and plain lifestyle, preference for English and Swiss-Palatine dialects over High German, and denominational dogmatism. To the Swiss and the *Kanadier*, the *Russländer* were too German, too progressive, too liberal, too educated, too aggressive, and too urban-oriented. These differences created much friction and mis-understanding and they epitomize the wide gulf in attitudes, outlook, and values that often separates two waves of immigrants from the same homeland, such as the pre-World War I and post-World War I generations of ethnic Germans.

CHAPTER XII

THE HUTTERITES

1. Colony life
2. Spatial expansion and reception
3. Migration to Canada
4. Origins and culture

Colony life

The German-speaking Hutterites are a deeply religious Christian group who migrated to western Canada in 1918. They believe that honouring God properly means to live and work communally, to practice pacifism, and to consider worldly life as a preparation for death and eternal life. They regard the laws of man as instruments of the devil and view public schools, taxes, courts, and government services with suspicion. Interpreting the Scriptures literally, they lead a simple and austere life, reject worldly fashions and private property, and practice religious communism according to Acts 11, 2:44: "And all that believe were together, and had all things in common. And sold their possessions and goods and parted them to all men, as every man had need." Hutterites do not know economic inequality or crime. They live in small, rural, farming colonies comprising 80 to 130 persons each where life is strictly ordered and regulated by the proper observance of religious practices. Young children are taught to pray, sing hymns, read, and write in German. They are thereby introduced to Hutterite beliefs and behaviour before they enter English schools. Hutterite schools are noted for their effective training of the young. Each family occupies separate living quarters in the colony, but all meals are prepared in the communal kitchen and eaten in the communal dining hall. The interior of their living quarters lacks modern conveniences and is as plain as their clothes, whose functional style dates back to their origins four centuries ago.

The Hutterite village-type communal colonies, known as *Bruderhöfe*, consist of barrack-like buildings, functionally designed and logically arranged. Church, school, communal kitchen, and dwelling houses are usually grouped in the centre of the colony. These are surrounded by barns, stables, sheds, shops, granaries, and vast fields of farmland on which a variety of products are raised, ranging from geese and cattle to fruit and grain. Each *Bruderhof* covers an average of 5,000 acres of land, owned collectively by its members. Despite their similarities to the Amish, the Hutterites reject the horse-and-buggy approach to farming and avail themselves of the most modern technology and most advanced agricultural methods. They operate a mixed-farm economy and produce most of their livestock feed. They erect their own buildings, repair their own equipment, and make their own clothes. Each woman receives a sewing machine as a wedding gift from the community. This makes them self-sufficient and largely independent from the outside world.

On each colony there is a strict division of labour. Jobs are not selected individually, but assigned in accordance with abilities and skills. The preacher, chosen by casting lots, is recognized as the colony's head. The *Wirt*, or boss, is the manager of all material needs. He administers the colony's money and assets and assigns the work. Stewards who are responsible for various types of economic activities assist the *Wirt* in the supervision of work. On large colonies there may be a pig boss, a chicken boss, a cattle boss, a head cook, a carpenter, a gardener, etc., each with a specific number of helpers assigned. Colonies have their own electricians, machinists, plumbers, engineers, and so on. No one is paid wages, but the basic wants and needs of all are looked after. Since the number of occupations is limited, a colony must divide from time to time. All profit is invested in new land, some of it acquired for the purpose of outfitting a daughter colony, as explained below.

Spatial expansion and reception

The Hutterites are the largest and the fastest growing family-type communal group known in the western world. Their international population grew from 1,500 in 1908 to 27,000 in 1987. More than two thirds of them live in western Canada and most of the remaining ones in the United States. Of the original 15 Canadian Hutterite colonies started in 1918, 9 were set up in Alberta and 6 in Manitoba, where by 1974 they had increased to 84 and 53 respectively. In 1987 Alberta's 170 *Bruderhöfe* occupied 1 percent of the arable land in that province. The Hutterites expand by forming daughter colonies whenever a parent colony reaches a size of 120-140 persons. This could happen as often as every 14 years.

Nativist sentiment combined with public fear of unlimited Hutterite growth has led to restrictive provincial legislation. In Alberta a 1942 law prohibited the sale of land to enemy aliens and Hutterites. A 1947 law regulated the acreage permissible per colony and the distance from each other. In 1960 another Alberta law made land sales to Hutterites conditional upon approval by a community property loan board and the provincial cabinet. Similar restrictions have been considered in Manitoba and Saskatchewan. The result has been a wide dispersion of Hutterite settlement in the West. Hutterites have been subjected to much overt discrimination in Canada because of their self-imposed isolation from society, their seemingly strange ways, their German language, and the success of their large-scale farming, regardless of drought, depression, or inflation. They have been accused of grabbing the best land, using religion to avoid taxation, and making a fortune in farming.

Migration to Canada

The first 1,000 Hutterites came to Canada in 1918 from South Dakota where all the Hutterites resided before World War I. After America entered the war in 1917, the American Hutterites were severely harassed and persecuted because the U.S. had no provision for conscientious objectors. Their refusal to be drafted, buy war bonds, and give up the German language made them subject to charges of pro-Germanism and to attacks by hostile neighbours. Some Hutterites were court-martialed and placed in barracks, while others were abused and publicly ridiculed. The property of colonies was vandalized and their cattle and sheep were stolen. The cruel torture of four forcibly drafted Hutterites with the resultant death of two of them triggered the decision of all of the 18 American Hutterite colonies to relocate to Canada.

The Hutterites were able to enter Canada on the basis of an Order-in-Council of 1899 that specifically granted them immunity from military service. In Alberta, however, public reaction was so hostile to the admission of these Germans who refused to engage in military service that in October 1918 the federal government was compelled to restrict immigration to Hutterites born in the United States, thereby excluding those born in Russia. Then in April 1919 the Canadian government rescinded the 1899 law. The continued agitation by the Great War Veterans Association finally resulted in the Order-in-Council of May 1919. That further prohibited all Hutterite and Mennonite immigration to Canada and thus prevented the last-18th-Hutterite colony from entering.

Origins and culture

The cultural and social peculiarities of the Hutterites are difficult to comprehend without a knowledge of their roots in the Protestant Reformation of 16th-century Germany. Together with the Mennonites and the Old Order Amish, the Hutterites are one of the three surviving Anabaptist groups who have attempted to establish voluntary Christian "communities of love" since the 1520's. "Anabaptism" means "rebaptism" and refers to their rejection of infant baptism in favour of adult baptism as the basis of a pure church of equals who are Christian by their own free decision. Taking the Scriptures literally, the members of such communities surrendered their earthly possessions, refused to participate in wars, and dissociated themselves from all existing institutions, including the official Catholic and Protestant state churches. As a result, they were persecuted and many became martyrs. One of their early leaders, Jacob Huter of Tyrol, was burnt at the stake in 1536.

Hutterites date their origin to 1528 when a group of Anabaptist refugees in Moravia introduced the practice of "community of goods." The early Hutterite communities consisted of Anabaptist refugees from Switzerland, southern Germany, and Austria. For a century they were able to develop some eighty prosperous Hutterite colonies in Protestant Moravia until they were decimated and expelled during the Thirty Years' War. In Moravia, Hutterites had become famous for their medical skills, literacy, and expertise in many trades ranging from ceramics and cutlery to clocks and carriage-making.

Their expulsion from Moravia in 1622 started a long trek of migrations eastward from 1621 to 1770, first to Slovakia, then to Hungary, Transylvania, and Wallachia, and finally to the Ukraine. In their search for a sanctuary they endured much suffering. A Jesuit campaign to restore the Catholic faith led to their near extermination in 1688 and only 44 families survived the flight to Russia. There they were left in peace for a century, achieving material recovery and experiencing religious revival. The Russian government's repeal in 1872 of the privileges and exemptions granted them earlier, especially the exemption from military service, prompted their decision to relocate the colonies to the United States. All Hutterites, numbering 800 persons, settled in South Dakota. The leaders of the first three colonies founded in America between 1874 and 1877 gave their names to the three different Hutterite groups which exist in North America today, the Schmiedeleut, Dariusleut and Lehrerleut.

CHAPTER XIII

THE WORLD WAR I EXPERIENCE

1. The destruction of German-Canadian cultural life
2. Internment, disenfranchisement, and deportation
3. Patterns of discrimination
4. The renaming of Berlin, Ontario

The destruction of German-Canadian cultural life

The First World War was the main watershed in the history of German Canadians. Germans, considered Canada's most desirable non-British citizens until the war, became the most undesirable ones overnight. The wartime propaganda image of the German and Austrian troops as barbarous "Huns" was transferred to German Canadians who became the convenient scapegoats for the hatreds and frustrations British Canadians experienced in four years of total war. All Canadians of German background, whether of *reichsdeutsche*, Austrian, or ethnic German origin, whether recent immigrants or the identifiable descendants of Germans who had come generations earlier, were stigmatized as "enemy aliens." Their culture, which had formed an integral part of the Canadian heritage from the beginning, was denounced as alien to Canada. Virtually all German ethnic associations were dissolved, German disappeared as a subject of study from schools and universities, and all German-language schools and many German churches were closed. Canada's German-language press was first censored, then suppressed. The importation of German-language books and newspapers was banned and new publications in the German language were not permitted until 1920.

Since German immigration was prohibited from 1914 until
1923, the vibrant and diverse German-Canadian cultural and
social life practically ceased and remained stifled throughout
the 1920's under the pressures of the Canadianization drive.
The habit of judging German Canadians according to
Canada's relations with Germany has become deeply ingrained
among British Canadians and has even defied the official
multiculturalism of the 1970's and 1980's. The systematic
deletion or omission from the country's historical record of
the contributions made by German settlers to the growth of
Canada is a legacy of World War I. In Canadian school texts,
government publications, and scholarly monographs, German
Canadians, if they are mentioned at all, are usually associated
with Germany's role in the two world wars.

Internment, disenfranchisement, and deportation

All Canadians whose mother tongue was German faced
severe government discrimination during the war. The War
Measures Act of August 1914 empowered the federal
government to censor all forms of communication and to
arrest, detain, and deport dangerous enemy aliens. An
Order-in-Council of October 1914 required all visitors and
landed immigrants from Germany and Austria-Hungary who
were not yet naturalized Canadian citizens to register with and
report monthly to a local magistrate, and surrender all
firearms. Enemy aliens considered dangerous were to be
interned in one of the twenty-four internment camps set up in
British Columbia, the Prairies, in northern Ontario, Quebec
and Nova Scotia. Official measures were determined as much
by the fear of a threat to Canada's security as by public
pressure.

Of 88,000 enemy aliens registered by the end of 1918, 8,600
were actually interned. Three thousand of these internees
were enemy reservists. The internees included 2,000 Germans,
6,000 Austro-Hungarians (including Croats, Ruthenians, Slo-
vaks, and Czechs), 200 Turks, and 100 Bulgarians. In 1916,
however, an acute manpower shortage led to the parole of
many internees. The maltreatment and unsanitary conditions
in the camps were so harsh that more than one hundred

internees died. Enemy aliens to be interned were often randomly selected, usually when they became unemployed or were denounced by overzealous patriots.

The increasingly vindictive atmosphere continued to be legally sanctioned even three months after the end of the war. A government decree in February 1919 provided that any person's complaint "evidencing a feeling of public apprehension entertained by the community" was sufficient cause for the internment of an enemy alien. The suspect enemy alien was neither entitled to legal counsel nor had the right to be informed of the proceedings against him. War hysteria reached its peak in early 1919 when the Canadian government gave serious consideration to petitions demanding the internment and mass expulsion of 85,000 registered enemy aliens. Only fear of the international repercussions and a shortage of transportation facilities reduced to 1,800 the number of those who were actually involuntarily repatriated to Europe between 1919 and 1920.

One of the most discriminatory measures enacted by the government against German Canadians was the Wartime Elections Act of September 1917. It denied the right to vote to all Canadian citizens who (1) claimed exemption from military service (this applied particularly to the Mennonites), (2) were born in an enemy country and naturalized after March 1902, and (3) were naturalized after March 1902 and whose mother tongue was the language of an enemy country. Swiss German immigrants were therefore also affected even though Switzerland had been neutral in World War I. Since a three-year residence was required before an immigrant was eligible for naturalization, this Act in fact disenfranchised the entire generation of German-speaking immigrants who arrived as long ago as 1899. It also created a legal precedent until 1977 for measures subjecting entire categories of naturalized citizens to the loss of their Canadian citizenship and their right to vote and to deportation. It legitimized the refusal of English Canadian judges to naturalize enemy aliens, regardless of the merits of their application, during both world wars.

Patterns of discrimination

The transformation of the trench war into a total war was paralleled by increasing discriminatory measures against enemy aliens on the home front. After the sinking of the Lusitania in May 1915 with the loss of some Canadian lives, English Canadians began to believe the much publicized British reports of alleged German atrocities in Belgium and to blame the war on everyone with a German background. As a result, Germans and Austrians were detained and interned on the slightest provocation. Private and public employers all over the country dismissed Germans and Austrians from their jobs, including naturalized senior municipal administrators (Dr. Erwin Kohlmann in Toronto), managers of public utilities (G.H. Glaubitz in London), and university professors. Athletes of German extraction were excluded from sports competitions. Toronto prohibited signs advertising German beer brewed in Berlin, Ontario, changed street names associated with Germans, and frowned upon the playing of German classical music. English Canadian judges ruled that enemy aliens did not have the right to apply to civil courts during the war. In February 1916 a group of prominent Canadians launched an Anti-German League in Toronto aimed at the dismissal of all Canadians of German or Austrian stock from public service and the elimination of German products, immigrants, and influence from Canada.

In 1916 anti-German sentiment escalated into acts of violence and the destruction of property associated with enemy aliens. In Victoria, Leiser's wholesale bakery was raided and the *Kaiserhof* hotel was destroyed by a mob in the hundreds. The B.C. Lieutenant Governor's wife who was of German descent was threatened. In Calgary a hotel and a restaurant that hired Germans were wrecked by a mob of 1,500 and local ethnic Germans feared for their lives. In Montreal a club was destroyed. In Berlin a Lutheran pastor who preached in German was dragged from his house into the street by a band of soldiers, and Concordia Hall was broken into twice and completely ransacked by an unruly mob led by soldiers.

By the end of the war a new stereotype of the German Canadian emerged. This was a foreigner incapable of loyalty to Canada and unassimilable. Derogatory labels such as "Huns" and "Bohunks" abounded in the popular literature of the time. Writers like the Reverend Wellington Bridgman charged that Germans and Austrians were capable of "unnameable treachery and crime" and demanded that all "Huns" and "Austro-Huns" be dispossessed and deported for the benefit of English Canadian war veterans. The discriminatory and racist immigration legislation of 1919 and the prohibition of German, Austrian, Mennonite, and Hutterite immigration by Order-in-Council in 1919 reflected prevailing opinion. Unable to defend themselves against discrimination, insults, and abuse in the media and by public speakers, many German Canadians assumed a Dutch or Scandinavian identity.

The renaming of Berlin, Ontario

Naturalized German Canadians were totally helpless in the face of arbitrary disenfranchisement and too intimidated to protest against discrimination. The unilateral and often deliberately provocative renaming of well-established German place names in eastern and western Canada have left to posterity permanent reminders of the prevalent mood among British Canadians towards fellow Canadians and their heritage. In western Canada names of places settled by German immigrants were changed as follows: Coblenz to Cavell, Kaiser to Peebles, Prussia to Leader, Waldorf to Béthune, Carlstadt to Alderson, Wittenberg to Leedale, and Düsseldorf to Freedom.

The best known case involved the imposition of the name of Kitchener on the Ontario town of Berlin, the prosperous manufacturing city and traditional centre of German settlement in central Canada. From the beginning of the war the citizens of Berlin had gone to great pains to demonstrate their loyalty to Canada's cause. For instance, throughout the war, Berlin and neighbouring Waterloo surpassed other regions of Canada in contributions to patriotic fund drives. In addition, about 10 percent of the 2,800 volunteers from Waterloo County's population of 70,000 died in battle.

The renaming resulted from two separate ballots in May and June 1916: after the first one, the name Berlin was dropped, after the second one, the name Kitchener was adopted. The proposal was sprung on the public in February 1916 by an anonymous "ratepayer" without any previous discussion. Alleged atrocities committed by the German Empire inspired the chief arguments for a name change. The allegations widely circulated in Canada of German atrocities were too obviously one-sided to be entirely credible, even in 1916. Indeed, they were later revealed to have been British fabrications. But since such doubts could not be aired freely, the arguments in favor of changing Berlin's name were irrefutable. Opposition to a name change by many prominent Berliners was stifled by anti-German riots. Fewer than half of the 1,080 signatures on a petition demanding a change came from eligible voters, and some of their signatures were said to have been extorted "through dread of raids" on their business establishments. With many opponents to a change not voting on the first referendum in May 1916 for fear of reprisals and the deliberate misrepresentation of their motives, those in favor of change won by a majority of 83 out of 3,075 ballots cast.

The electorate for the May 1916 ballot included large numbers of previously non-resident proponents of change and excluded, as a citizens' petition of July 1916 addressed to the Government of Ontario charged, "scores of opponents who had lived here for decades... [and] had voted at every parliamentary and municipal election in all these years." The petition was signed by 2,068 Berlin residents -- nearly six times the number of votes cast in the second referendum in June 1916 in support of the name Kitchener. Although endorsed by the town council of Waterloo, the petition was rejected by the government of Ontario. When the petition was published under the title "The Other Side, An Appeal for British Fair Play" the press ridiculed it as "so much piffle."

The second ballot in June 1916 offered the voters a choice of six unattractive names, after the popular option of amalgamation with Waterloo had been undemocratically eliminated. Kitchener was chosen by 8 percent of the electorate with only 18 percent of eligible voters participating. The new name was put forward three weeks before the referendum after it was learned that the popular British military figure, General Kitchener, had drowned as his ship was sunk by the German

Navy. Since public opposition to the change-of-name movement was interpreted as disloyalty and pro-Germanism, the outcome of the referendum was a foregone conclusion. Attempts in 1919 to restore the name of Berlin by plebiscite were nipped in the bud by the Great War Veterans' Association.

Some historians, ignoring the prevailing wartime atmosphere of Germanophobia, intolerance, and intimidation, have suggested that Berlin residents of German descent desired the name change, that it was democratically implemented, and that it was timely. To be sure, a minority of local merchants and manufacturers of German extraction supported the British League's campaign to get rid of the name Berlin. For profit-conscious businesspeople the trademark "Made in Berlin" was a financial liability in 1916. But evidence abounds that most Berliners -- 70 percent of the city's residents claimed German descent -- objected to the manner in which their town's name was deleted, and most did not like to have the name Kitchener forced on them. To them the entire campaign of 1916 was aimed at demoralizing German Canadians and discrediting their heritage. On July 26, 1916, under the title "What's in a Name?", the *Berliner Journal* mustered the courage to publish the following revealing sentiment: "A name established, like that of Berlin for 90 years, has become part of civic consciousness. To change it is to produce a feeling of unnaturalness among those citizens especially who, with their fathers before them, have dwelt in the place for generations. To such persons the place under the new name will never seem quite the same. They have been robbed of part of their being. This, and not because there is a Berlin in Germany, was the real reason for the opposition to a change in Berlin's name."

CHAPTER XIV

ON THE EVE OF WORLD WAR I

1. Patterns of settlement
2. Cultural diversity
3. Ethnic pride and public recognition
4. Economic strength

Patterns of settlement

On the eve of the First World War, German Canadians formed a proud and integral part of Canadian society. Dispersed across Canada from coast to coast, their different patterns of settlement reflected the diversity of their cultural backgrounds and their adaptation to a variety of socio-economic and geographic conditions. They lived in rural and urban areas, in closed settlements and in ethnically mixed districts, on solitary farmsteads and at the frontier of civilization in the northern wilderness, in denominationally homogeneous blocks, and in small towns whose founders had immigrated from Germany generations ago. The 1911 Census counted 400,000 people of German descent in Canada, which was 5.6 percent of the Canadian population.

In Atlantic Canada the largest concentration (39,000) of Canadians of German descent was found in Nova Scotia, primarily in Lunenburg and Halifax counties, where they formed 8 percent of the population. About 3,200 were in southeastern New Brunswick and 6,200 in southwestern Quebec. Since most of these were the descendants of immigrants who had arrived generations ago, fewer than 2 percent of the total population, mostly in the cities of Montreal, Halifax, and Lunenburg, were able to speak

German. Canada's largest prewar German community (200,000) was in Ontario where it formed 8 percent of the population. The centres of German settlement were southwestern Ontario, especially Waterloo County (37,000), and the Niagara district (20,000), but German was no longer spoken in the latter. Although the origins of both date back a century, Waterloo County had retained its German character because of the continued influx of newcomers from Germany who coexisted harmoniously with the original Pennsylvania German Mennonite settlers. On the other hand, the Niagara district had, at the same time, attracted large numbers of non-German immigrants, a factor resulting in the linguistic assimilation of its original German settlers. Except for Berlin (Kitchener) with a population of 11,000 Germans and Toronto with 9,000 Germans, most Ontario Germans formed rural-urban communities in or near small towns.

German settlement patterns in western Canada differed considerably from those in eastern Canada for two main reasons: (1) geography and (2) the predominantly east European origins of the German settlers. In Manitoba 42,000 German-speakers formed 8 percent of the population. The largest groups were the 15,000 Mennonites from Russia, who lived in one of the most prosperous and uniquely laid-out closed "reserves" on the Prairies, and the 14,000 Germans in urban Winnipeg. Saskatchewan's 70,000 Germans represented 14 percent of that province's population. There, 12,000 German Catholics lived in two Catholic block settlements. However, most of the Saskatchewan Germans had settled in a large number of smaller and denominationally more or less homogeneous Catholic, Mennonite, and Protestant colonies. In Alberta 37,000 predominantly Lutheran settlers of German descent made up 10 percent of the population. All of these were farmers who had settled in denominational patterns, except for the nearly 6,000 German residents of Calgary and Edmonton. In British Columbia, Victoria and Vancouver Island had become a preferred destinations for *Reichsdeutsche*, among them prominent speculators such as Alvo von Alvensleben, who promoted an active secular cultural life.

Cultural diversity

Basic to any understanding of the sizable and widely
dispersed German-Canadian population on the eve of the
First World War is an understanding of its cultural diversity.
This was the decisive factor that shaped relations among
German Canadians as well as relations between them and
non-German groups. Unlike the post-World War I immigrants, most pre-World War I German-speaking immigrants
had a weakly developed German national consciousness, if any
at all. In contrast to German Americans, the pre-World War I
German-Canadian settlers founded few secular clubs. Instead,
Canada's German-speaking immigrants during the period
1870-1914 gave their first allegiance to their church or
denomination. This expressed itself in their settlement
patterns, their support of voluntary associations, and in their
desire to preserve German traditions and values through
schools, publications, or cultural activities. Individual German
denominational groups related to Canada and to other groups
in different ways and frequently subordinated common
German linguistic and cultural interests to denominational
objectives.

The reasons for this must be attributed largely to the fact
that in western Canada -- the primary destination of German
immigration in the four decades before the outbreak of World
War I -- only 12 percent of the German-speaking settlers were
natives of Germany. Germans from eastern Europe made up
70 percent of western Canada's new German community.
Most of the remaining German settlers were second to fourth
generation German Americans. Among eastern Europe's
Germans, ethnicity in combination with religious creed had
been the strongest, if not the sole, influence on community
formation. The church congregation had been the only form
of cultural association and it satisfied religious as well as
social needs. In the vast rural areas of eastern Europe, where
German colonies were scattered among Russians, Poles,
Ukrainians, Hungarians, Romanians, and other people, the
church congregation had kept the German language and
culture alive. It would be only natural that emigrants would
transplant the life and settlement patterns already known to
them to Canada.

The huge influx of east European Germans into the newly opened territories of western Canada added new stones to the mosaic of the older, culturally already very diverse, German-Canadian community in eastern Canada. There was little social and cultural interaction among Germans from eastern Europe and from Germany, Russian and Swiss Mennonites, German Baptists and Amish, Lutherans and Reformed believers, Protestants and Catholics, Lunenburg Germans and Waterloo County Germans, Austrians and Swiss, etc. Even communication in German was often difficult, if not impossible, among those who spoke Low German, Swiss, Palatine, Swabian, Saxon, and other old German accents and dialects which had been curiously preserved in the linguistic isolation of the diaspora. These groups tended to be disinterested in identifying with other German Canadians as a group. For instance, not until 1913 was an attempt made in Winnipeg to form a German-Canadian National Association as an umbrella organization of German Canadians, even though various German secular clubs existed there.

Ethnic pride and public recognition

The unabashed and naive pride which German Canadians displayed prior to 1914 in their cultural heritage and ethnic identity is difficult to imagine today in view of the experiences and lessons of two world wars. They knew no problems of dual identity and conflicts of divided loyalty; in fact, they publicly advertised themselves as being among Canada's best, most successful, and most loyal citizens. In Berlin (Kitchener), Ontario, the ethnic pride of the majority of its residents manifested itself in the uninhibited, annual celebration of Kaiser William's birthday and in the singing, on official occasions, of the city's dual anthem *"Die Wacht am Rhein"* and "God save the King." Berlin's annual *Sängerfeste*, which attracted participants even from the United States, and such festivals as the *Kirmes* were expressions of self-confidence in the harmony of German traditions with Canadian life. Ontario's German-language press abounded with sentimental adulations of the German fatherland and its rulers while, at the same time, giving unswerving loyalty to Canada. German-speaking religious groups like the Mennonites, Amish, and

Moravians, as well as individual businessmen and political representatives, like Adam Beck and Member of Parliament H.H. Miller, had no qualms about the duality of their loyalty leading to conflict of interest. Even assimilated descendants of settlers from diverse German backgrounds liked to take pride in their German roots.

Public recognition of the accomplishments of Germans in the development of Canada and widespread social acceptance of German settlers by the English-speaking host society was the complement to German ethnic pride. Almost without exception, Canadian politicians, statesmen, and writers expressed their appreciation for the German settlers' qualities. The well-known Protestant missionary James S. Woodsworth summed up prevailing British-Canadian opinion when he asserted that despite their clubs and newspapers, Germans were easily assimilated. They did not form a distinct class and were classified as "white people like ourselves" even by those who detested "foreigners." As late as May 1914 the Governor General of Canada publicly admired the traits of this "great Teutonic race" which would "go far in the making of good Canadians and loyal citizens of the British Empire." Participation of German Canadians in political life encountered few difficulties and Germans played prominent roles at the municipal, provincial, and federal levels in areas where Germans had settled. English Canadians applauded and frequently attended cultural activities of their fellow German citizens in Ontario and in the urban communities of the West. Canadian historians, in sharp contrast to the situation after 1914, eagerly researched and featured the prominent role of German pioneers in the opening up and settling of Canada.

Economic strength

Public recognition was facilitated by the fact that the contributions of German Canadians, unlike those of the French Canadians, were primarily economic in nature. The German-Canadian MP Miller (South Grey) admitted in 1908 that "the German in Canada does not hold quite so tenaciously, it may be, to the use of the language of his fathers as do our French-Canadian friends" and, he went on, whatever their position in life, "the German people are brought up to work, and they all work, and are characteristically industrious." By 1914 their reputation as successful farmers in North America was well established. The model farms of the German Mennonites from Russia on prairie virgin land were widely admired and praised.

The success of German-Canadian manufacturers and businessmen was equally proven and not only in the area of Waterloo County, Ontario. They excelled, for example, in the production of quality musical instruments, as names like Theodor Heintzman and A.& S. Nordheimer (both Toronto) attest. Toronto, Ottawa, Hamilton, Montreal, and Winnipeg had sizable German communities whose members played prominent roles in the economic and cultural lives of these cities. In Winnipeg, for instance, Joseph Hecker founded western Canada's first Philharmonic Society in 1880, and in Toronto Dr. Augustus Vogt launched the famous Mendelsohn Choir in 1884. Germans had a reputation for working harder than their fellow workers and causing fewer problems for their employers. This is attributed to their aspiration to become the employers of tomorrow. Most German Canadians, whether as farmers, skilled workers, or businessmen, were at least as prosperous as the average Canadian. German workers typically owned their own attractive homes that were surrounded by well-cultivated fruit and vegetable gardens. In the newly opened western territories, German settlers encountered relatively fewer difficulties in securing an economic base than other groups of settlers.

CHAPTER XV

PIONEERS IN BRITISH COLUMBIA

1. Discoverers and founding fathers
2. The gold rush
3. Count Constantion Alvo von Alvensleben
4. German cultural and social life

Discoverers and founding fathers

Among the four western Canadian provinces, British Columbia could claim the smallest but oldest and most colourful German presence by 1914. Germans were among the first Europeans to explore the resources of the land. Captain Cook's ill-fated "Voyage of Discovery" of 1778, which marked the beginning of a fur trade in the territory, included at least one, and possibly two, Germans. Heinrich Zimmermann, who is identified as the first German to set foot on B.C., published his account of the Cook expedition in 1781 in Germany. In the following 70 years German scientists, explorers, and travellers, such as the naturalist Berthold Seemann, were reported to have visited this territory which then contained no white settlements. In the early 1840's the government of Prussia considered the desirability of acquiring neighbouring California from Mexico for trade and settlement but decided that the cost of controlling the hostile native people and the advancing American settlers would be too high.

Until 1858 the territory of what became B.C. was governed by the Hudson's Bay Company. The first prominent settler of German background was the Hudson's Bay Company physician, Dr. John Sebastian Helmcken, who arrived in 1850 with the first group of colonists. Helmcken, born in London in 1825 of parents who had come from Hannover, Germany, was fluent in English and German. Appointed magistrate of Fort Rupert on Vancouver Island, he was responsible for the defence of the white settlers against the hostile Indians. In 1855 Helmcken was elected to the first colonial legislature. As the leader of the delegation that negotiated Confederation with Canada in 1870, he was one of the founding fathers of the Province of British Columbia.

The gold rush

The most powerful incentive for the beginning of permanent white settlement and for the establishment of the colony of British Columbia in 1858 was the lure of gold. It attracted settlers and prospectors, many of whom were German, northward from California where the discovery of gold in 1849 had greatly accelerated immigration. With the Cariboo gold strike of 1858 the rush of prospectors from California to the Fraser River Valley was on. A high percentage of Germans were among the first party of 500 diggers from San Francisco in March 1858 and among the subsequent waves of miners. The census of 1881 recorded 858 Germans in a population of 24,000 non-native residents, which made Germans the fourth largest immigrant group after British, Asians, and French.

In 1858 the Governor of the colony was alarmed at the sudden influx of what he termed "the very dregs of society." They were certainly different from the type of settlers who had opened up eastern Canada and who were to civilize the prairies a few decades later. The gold seekers were restless adventurers who did not come to settle down in order to pursue a steady trade or occupation.

The memories of B.C.'s gold rush days abound with the antics of its many German pioneer prospectors. For instance, in 1861 the finds of three Germans led by Bill Dietz started a second gold rush in the Cariboo district. However "Dutch Bill" didn't dig deep enough and others made their fortune on William's Creek, named after him. The Bavarian Ned Stout was almost killed by Indians while searching for gold and proudly showed off his scars until his dying day in 1924. Another Bavarian, Frank Laumeister, became first a laughing stock and later a legendary figure for his unsuccessful importation of camels from California as freight carriers. In 1861 Augustus Schubert from Dresden, his pregnant wife, and their three children pioneered the first overland journey from Winnipeg to the gold fields. Instead of lasting the anticipated sixty days, their trip turned into a seven-months' struggle for survival. Other German prospectors devised different profit-generating ventures, such as importing dancing girls from Berlin to act as "hurdy-gurdies."

As the supply centre for the gold rush, Victoria became the first permanent white settlement. Many Germans left the lure of the gold to become suppliers, ranchers, and businessmen. Others took up logging, lumbering, grain milling, and farming. They stood out as successful settlers and were prominent as community leaders, brewers, bakers, furniture makers, iron founders, cigar makers, wholesale suppliers, etc. They participated actively in the speculation and investment activities which fuelled the province's burgeoning economic growth. In the rapidly rising financial and commercial capital of Vancouver, David Oppenheimer, a native of Frankfurt-on-Main, was elected the second mayor in 1888. He and other German pioneer businessmen, such as the Grauers from Württemberg, did much to promote the economic development of Vancouver.

Gustav Constantin Alvo von Alvensleben

One of the most colourful German residents of Vancouver was the son of Count Werner Alvo von Alvensleben, a prominent Prussian nobleman. Young Alvo's escapades as a cadet in the German army had made him the black sheep of the family. In 1904 his father gave him the choice of either reforming himself in a remote garrison or resigning as an officer. Alvo requested free passage to America and arrived in Vancouver with 4 dollars in his pocket. For one year he earned his livelihood as a farmhand, painter, fisherman, and nightwatchman. The next year he bought his own fishing boat and started a chicken and dairy peddling business. As a real estate broker he benefitted from Vancouver's spectacular boom in 1908 and rose to become one of the must successful stock market and investment speculators. Tapping the capital of wealthy investors in the German Empire, he is reputed to have invested 7 million dollars into the B.C. economy. Alvensleben advanced to become one of Canada's foremost entrepreneurs where he entailed respect and acceptance by Canada's and Germany's social elites. *Who's Who in Canada* devoted a full page to Alvensleben. Among his German investors were the German Imperial Chancellor von Bethmann-Hollweg and Kaiser William II. In 1912 he was at the peak of his career but when World War I broke out, his enterprises went into steep decline. Declared an "Enemy of the Dominion," he was prohibited from entering Canada from 1914 to 1929, and his Canadian assets were confiscated by the Crown. After unsuccessful attempts to rebuild his business in Seattle, he was interned in the United States as an enemy alien from 1917-1920. He died a poor and forgotten man in Seattle in 1965, 86 years old.

Alvensleben's upward social mobility and his civic record is no less legendary than his financial success. He gave countless lavish parties in his splendid Vancouver residence, supported the arts and other public causes, and was generally liked and admired. The *Deutsche Klub* he organized was patronized by virtually every German in Vancouver, as well as by Englishmen. He developed "Wigwam Inn" at the foot of Mount Dickens into a luxurious fresh air spa where splendid, much discussed garden parties were held with German food, German bands, dancing, and moonlight yacht cruises.

German cultural and social life

The *Deutsche Klub* in Vancouver did not provide the only centre of German social and cultural activity in B.C. In Victoria a *Germania Sing Verein* was formed as early as 1861 and lasted up to 1914. It was the first cultural association in B.C. The sizable German presence in Victoria prompted schools to teach German, along with Spanish, French, Greek, and Latin. Victoria's German community, which in 1870 favored B.C.'s annexation by the United States, put on lavish ceremonies on Kaiser William's and Queen Victoria's birthdays. The death of Kaiser William I in 1888 was celebrated by the *Liederkranz* Society with an elaborate mourning service

which was attended by English fellow-citizens. In 1892
German businessmen in Vancouver launched the first Canadian chapter of the *Hermannssöhne*, or Sons of Hermann
Lodge. It became deeply involved in community life and
organized many activities. Two German-language newspapers
were founded in Vancouver: the *Westliche Kanadische Post* in
1906 and the bilingual *Vancouver German Press* in 1911.
B.C.'s pre-World War I German community consisted predominantly of natives of Germany, most of whom had entered
the province via the United States. In the 1920's and 1930's
Russländer Mennonite and Sudeten German refugees found
a haven in B.C., as did *Volksdeutsche* who were suffering from
the drought and Depression in Alberta and Saskatchewan.

CHAPTER XVI

PIONEERS IN ALBERTA

1. The first German-speaking settlers
2. The mass influx from 1896 to 1914
3. Urban communities

The first German-speaking settlers

Alberta, separated by the Rocky Mountains from British Columbia, was the last Canadian province settled by immigrants. A main reason for its late settlement was that the challenges of climate, aridity, and isolation demanded unique qualities of adaptation, ingenuity, and endurance from pioneers.

Following Confederation in 1867, Canada was eager for immigrant settlers to fill the sparsely populated area known at the time as the Northwest Territories. (Alberta was carved out of this in 1905.) Canada realized that settlers were necessary in order to create a transcontinental nation and prevent an American takeover of unsettled land. Immigration, however, remained negligible until 1896, when Minister of the Interior Clifford Sifton, a member of the newly elected Liberal government in Ottawa, launched an aggressive promotion campaign in Europe and the United States. Prior to 1896, a number of factors had combined to discourage settlement in Alberta: Anglo-Canadian ranchers in southern Alberta had opposed farming because of the restrictions it would place on freely grazing cattle, cheap land had been available for farmers in the United States, and there had been a widespread apprehension that southern Alberta's dry climate made it unsuitable for farming.

When settlers nonetheless began arriving in Alberta, German-speaking people were among the earliest farming pioneers. In 1882 two Germans, Gustav Neumann and Carl Schoening, settled in Pincher Creek in the southwestern corner of the province. Two years later more German Lutherans joined them. In 1885 the district of Medicine Hat, two years after its formation, counted 19 residents of German origin among its population of 732. South of Medicine Hat, a party of 630 Germans from Galicia started a second string of colonies in 1889 and laid the foundation for a large settlement of German origin. In 1891, however, two years of unanticipated drought forced most of these settlers to relocate near Edmonton. There, German Lutherans from Galicia founded Hoffnungsau and Rosenthal near Stony Plain, German Reformed from Galicia founded Josephsberg near Fort Saskatchewan, and German Lutherans from Russia founded Heimthal and Lutherhort, i.e., present-day Ellerslie, in Rabbit Hills. In 1893 German Baptists from Volhynia settled in Leduc district and in 1894 Germans from the Moravian Church in Volhynia started Brüderheim and Brüderfeld colonies near Edmonton. From 1893 German Americans settling in Red Deer, Wetaskiwin, and Leduc pioneered large-scale American migrations to western Canada, while Galicia Germans were instrumental in inducing Ukrainian migrations to Canada. As a result of migrations prior to 1896, the triangle Edmonton-Wetaskiwin-Camrose was first settled by German-speaking people.

The mass influx from 1896 to 1914

The successful rural districts south and west of Edmonton became strongholds of German settlement in Alberta after 1896 because they attracted more German-speaking coreligionists. Continued German-speaking migrations into the area along the C.P.R. line Wetaskiwin-Edmonton gave settlers of German origin, despite heavy Scandinavian, British, and Ukrainian in-migration, predominance in eleven adjoining townships around Leduc by 1911 and made this the largest area of German settlement in Alberta. From 1897 on, the economically flourishing settlements near Stony Plain and Golden Spike drew a steady stream of German Lutheran settlers from Galicia, Volhynia, and other parts of Russia. North and northwest of Edmonton, Russian Mennonites began to move into Mellowdale (1908), Reformed Church Volga Germans settled near Mellowdale (1897), and *Reichs-deutsche* near Düsseldorf and Barrhead (1909) as well as along the railway line to the Peace River (1913). The Barrhead area, however, became a centre of German settlement only after World War I.

Between 1901 and 1911 Alberta's population of German origin, according to the census, grew from 7,836 to 41,656 and constituted 11 percent of the total population. With the addition of Russian and other east European Germans whose ethnic origin the census confused with their country of last permanent residence, the total German-origin population was well over 50,000. This was reflected in the German names given to twenty-six towns or post offices and twenty school districts. German settlers opened nearly ninety previously unsettled districts in every part of Alberta and in the process introduced ten new German-American religious denominations. Mennonites from Ontario and the United States started several colonies near Didsbury after 1900. German-American Catholics moved into the Pincher Creek area in 1896 and into the Spring Lake area in 1902. Rosenheim originated in 1911 as an extension of the German Catholic St. Joseph's colony in Saskatchewan. The large German migration to the Peace River district did not start until 1916 and the Hutterite influx not until 1918.

Urban communities

Although the federal government wanted to recruit only farmers as settlers for the prairies, German-speaking immigrants formed a sizable portion of the growing industrial labour force in Alberta's industries, such as the coal mines of Lethbridge and Medicine Hat. In Edmonton, Calgary, and Medicine Hat, German workers developed their own distinct neighbourhoods. In these cities and in the towns located in or near German settlements, German-speaking merchants and entrepreneurs played a visible role. Between 1900 and 1914 the colourful career of German immigrant Alfred Freiherr

von Hammerstein in many ways resembles that of his
contemporary Alvo von Alvensleben in British Columbia (see
chapter XV). He advanced from being a penniless Athabasca
River boy to founder of the *Alberta Herold* in 1903 and
became a pioneer developer of the Alberta tarsands. In 1909
he launched the Athabasca Oil and Asphalt Company with a
capital of 5 million dollars. Hammerstein, who died in 1941 in
Alberta, promoted a rail link from the American border to
Fort McMurray via Edmonton and the Peace River Crossing
and was one of the largest real estate owners in northern
Alberta. A no less illustrious entrepreneur was Martin
Nordegg from Silesia. In 1906, at the age of 38, he came to
Canada to explore its resources in response to a special
invitation from one of Sir Wilfred Laurier's personal friends.
With indefatigable energy and the German capital of his
Deutsches Canada Syndicate and German Development
Company Ltd. he developed Albertan coal deposits. Kaiser
William II decorated him on a visit to Berlin in 1910.

The cultural and social life of the urban German
communities manifested itself in the upsurge of secular
associations and a German-language press. Club *Harmonie* in
Calgary, organized in 1906 and succeeded by *Deutscher
Verein Frohsinn* in 1912, was Alberta's first German club. In
Edmonton the founding of Club *Edelweiss* by *Reichsdeutsche*
in 1905 was followed by the formation of a *Gesangverein
Germania* in 1908, a German Liberal Association in 1909, a
Deutscher Kranken-Unterstützungsverein in 1911, and a
Jung-Deutschland-Verein in 1913. The *Bund der Deutschen* in
Alberta was established in 1913 as the province-wide umbrella
organization. There were five German-language weeklies
founded: in Edmonton the *Alberta Herold* (1903), the *Alberta
Deutsche Zeitung*, and the *Farmer Freund* (both 1910), and in
Calgary *Der Deutsch-Canadier* and the *Deutsch-Canadischer
Farmer* (both 1909).

Secular entertainment organized by the clubs and newspa-
pers included German concerts, picnics, theatre, parades, and
similar activities. Germans benefitted from the fact that
Anglo-Canadians considered them, next to the British and
Americans, to be among the most preferred settlers in pioneer
Alberta. Acceptance by the host society facilitated assimilation

and vice versa. There were virtually no negative public comments about them prior to 1914, and in 1901 MP Frank Oliver, who was also editor of the *Edmonton Bulletin*, characterized the German immigrant as "a man of dominant race, of untiring energy, of great foresight; he is a man of sterling honesty and reliability... of the highest character."

CHAPTER XVII

PIONEERS IN SASKATCHEWAN

1. The Protestant pioneers
2. The Mennonite block settlements
3. The Catholic block settlements

The Protestant pioneers

Since its opening up to white settlement in the 1880's, Saskatchewan's proportion of residents of German origin has been the highest of any Canadian province. Census data of 1911 indicate that by 1914, 15 percent of the Saskatchewan population was German, making Germans after British the largest ethnic group in the province. If allowance is made for the erroneous classification of Russian and Austrian Germans this figure rises possibly up to 20 percent. As in Alberta, the fertile prairie and so-called parkland (mixed grass and forest zone) became accessible with the construction of the transcontinental railway in the early 1880's. Large-scale settlement, however, did not take place until the late 1890's when the Laurier government, in collaboration with the Canadian Pacific Railway (CPR), actively recruited farmers in central and eastern Europe. By that time, too, the last of the good, cheap land in the United States was gone. German settlers were attracted to the vast expanses of the Canadian virgin prairies by the government's offer of free land and freedom from military service, as well as its apparent tolerance of their language and culture.

Among the first European immigrants to Saskatchewan were natives of Germany. In 1884 and 1885, through the efforts and with the help of the CPR, they took up homesteads in places they named Strassburg (first named Neu Elsass) and Langenburg (first named Hohenlohe). The federal government was confident at the time that "the greater portion of the country north of Regina will, ere long, be filled with a population that will...reflect great credit upon the 'Vaterland'." However, emigration from Germany ceased, and the districts around Regina were settled instead by Germans from eastern Europe. Edenwold (first Neu Tulcea, then Edenwald), the second oldest German settlement in Saskatchewan, was started by Danube Swabians from the Bukovina (Romania). Between 1889 and 1904 the area northeast of Regina and around Melville filled up with Germans of the Lutheran and Reformed faiths from such different parts of eastern Europe as South Russia, the Volga region, Poland, Galicia, Volhynia, Courland (today's western Latvia), and Bessarabia.

Once settlement of the first pioneers had proven successful, migrations continued in family units. Close kinship, religious ties, and a supportive tradition of mutual assistance helped them survive the initial rigours of pioneering life. Edenwold, Langenburg, Lemberg, and Neudorf became waystations for chain migrations from various regions of eastern Europe and, occasionally, also from Germany. Typically, the newcomers worked for a while on the farms of their well-established countrymen and coreligionists in the Saskatchewan colonies until they had acquired the ways and means to start their own farms in daughter colonies. Thus, scattered colonies of German Protestants appeared after 1900 in central, northern, and southeastern Saskatchewan, often next to German Mennonite and Catholic block settlements.

The Mennonite block settlements

Population pressure among the Mennonites who had settled in Manitoba in the 1870's and their offspring's search for new land in the United States and in the Canadian prairies, prompted the Canadian government to reserve two sizable areas for them in Saskatchewan. It was done in collaboration with the CPR, which in 1890 had opened the line from Regina to Saskatoon. This step was an exception to the Canadian immigration policy that favoured the deliberate dispersal of settlers because it wanted to avoid the formation of non-

English ethnic communities. In Manitoba the Mennonites had proven themselves to be exemplary pioneers whom Canada could not afford to lose. The area in the Saskatchewan Valley to be settled by Mennonites had been rocked in 1885 by a serious uprising of Indians and Métis. Pacification of the prairies and establishment of firm Canadian control over the Northwest Territories, from which Saskatchewan created in 1905, depended on the stabilizing influence of permanent, large-scale, agricultural settlement.

The largest area reserved for a block settlement comprised five townships near Rosthern between the North and the South Saskatchewan Rivers. The initial settlers who arrived from Manitoba in 1892 were soon joined by Mennonite immigrants from Danzig (Germany) and Russia and by wealthy Mennonites from the U.S.A., whose parents had left Russia in the 1870's. It did not take long for Rosthern to acquire its reputation as one of the best and most profitable wheat-growing regions in Canada. By 1911, the predominantly German settlement around Rosthern had expanded to a block of 42 adjoining townships. Of its 8,000 German-speaking settlers, 800 were German Lutherans from Russia. Smaller Mennonite colonies near Herbert and Swift Current were started in 1903 by immigrants from Russia and the U.S.A. Conservative Mennonite congregations established themselves in their traditional village pattern, 17 at Rosthern and 15 near Swift Current. Thus, their pioneering efforts and religious cohesion had a supportive structure. The farmers had to travel such distances to their faraway fields, however, that villages proved inefficient and were later abandoned by most Mennonites in favour of single homestead farms.

The Catholic block settlements

The largest German block settlements in western Canada were the last to be started. These were the German-American Catholic colonies of St. Peter's and St. Joseph's in Saskatchewan. St. Peter's colony, covering an area of fifty townships around Humboldt and Muenster, was founded in 1902 as a result of the initiatives of Benedictine monks from Minnesota and Illinois. Their aim was to funnel the growing stream of

Catholic German Americans heading for the Canadian prairies into closed settlements. American experience had shown that ethnic block settlements would facilitate pastoral care and would better enable the clergy to preserve the immigrants' Catholic faith. The retention of the immigrant's native Catholic faith, it was assumed, was tied to the retention of the mother tongue.

Settlement began immediately after the Catholic Settlement Society had advertised the project in German-American newspapers and a Father Doerfler had selected a suitable spot on the Hoodoo Plains. A German-American land company was formed for the purpose of acquiring 108,000 acres of contiguous land and reselling it to suitable settlers. By 1914 St. Peter's colony had 8,000 German-Catholic settlers and all the good land was taken up. Most of the settlers were second-generation German Americans whose parents had immigrated from Germany and South Russia to Minnesota, the Dakotas, Wisconsin, and Kansas. They brought their cattle, machines, and household goods with them. About 10 percent of the settlers came directly from Germany and a few families arrived from South Russia and the Banat.

The spectacularly speedy and successful development of St. Peter's colony encouraged its organizers to acquire land in 1904 for a second closed colony. Although the colony was envisaged to include more than two hundred townships, government officials would assist in the acquisition of a block of only seventy-seven townships to be called St. Joseph's colony. The Catholic Colonization Association selected the treeless, open prairie west of Tramping Lake for St. Joseph's location and advertised the project in Russia and the U.S.A. Germans from Russia were accustomed to farming on similar land in the open Russian steppe. For wheat production they preferred it to the partially bush-covered terrain of St. Peter's colony. Spiritual care in St. Joseph's was in the hands of the German Brothers of the Oblate Order from Hünfeld, Germany. Between 1905 and 1914 nearly 8,000 German Catholic settlers filled fifty-five of the seventy-seven reserved townships. The German-American pioneers (whose parents had immigrated from South Russia and the Volga) were, after 1908, followed by a large influx of poverty-stricken Germans

from Russia. There were also numerous settlers from
Germany and various parts of Austria-Hungary. Leipzig, the
oldest district in the colony, was settled by equal numbers of
German Catholics from Russia, Germany, and Hungary.

Apart from these large block settlements, German Catholics
from different parts of Europe and the U.S.A. had established
smaller colonies in various parts of Saskatchewan. Josephstal,
the oldest one, was founded near Balgonie in 1886 by
Germans from Odessa (Russia). Due to continuing migrations
from South Russia, Balgonie became known in the 1890's as
the centre of German colonization in the Northwest and, by
1911, twenty townships in the area had been settled by
German Catholics. Germans from Romania, Austria-Hungary,
Germany, Ontario, and North Dakota established Catholic
colonies in the 1890's and around 1900 near Langenburg,
Grayson, Steelman, Estevan, Claybank, Allan, Quinton, and
Raymore. Since the homestead law made it difficult to farm
from European-style villages, the pioneer farmer often
depended on the church as his only cultural and social
contact. Church leaders encouraged and supported the
organization of denominationally homogeneous colonies. This
is one of the reasons predominantly rural regions, like
Saskatchewan, had few denominationally mixed settlements of
German-speaking immigrants exclusively from one specific
area of Germany, Austria, Russia, or Switzerland. Instead,
German-speaking newcomers from different parts of the world
did not mind associating with each other in new settlements as
long as all adhered to the same faith.

CHAPTER XVIII

PIONEERS IN MANITOBA

1. The opening of the West
2. The East and West Reserves
3. Non-Mennonite rural colonies
4. The significance of Winnipeg

The opening of the West

When the rights of the Hudson's Bay Company over the Northwest Territories were transferred to Canada in 1869, few considered the treeless prairie fit for agricultural use. In 1870, however, Manitoba was created as the first western Canadian province in order to forestall American designs on the empty Canadian virgin prairies. Now colonists were needed to pacify the rebellious Métis and to integrate Manitoba fully into Confederation. But settlement proceeded slowly and only along river valleys. No colonists dared to do without the water from rivers and the lumber from nearby forests. In fact, until 1874, no pioneers ventured to cultivate the open prairie. A project of 1872 by German-Canadian land surveyor William Wagner and the German Society of Montreal would have brought 50 families during 1873 and 100 families in 1874. But this attempt to recruit settlers in Germany had to be scrapped for lack of applicants, although the Dominion government had agreed in 1872 to put aside one and a half townships exclusively for German settlement.

Seven thousand German-speaking Mennonites from Russia became the trailblazers for the settlement of the western provinces when they accepted the challenge to prove the agricultural potential of the Canadian prairies. To these should go the credit for proving that successful farming on the open, treeless prairie was possible. Before they migrated from South Russia to Manitoba between 1874 and 1879, they had been farming the Russian steppe.

In a threefold manner the Mennonites pioneered the opening of the West. Most importantly by demonstrating that the prairies could be successfully farmed (which was not at all obvious before), they paved the way for others to follow as settlers on the vast, treeless grasslands of the West. They proved settlers from the steppe lands of eastern Europe to be particularly suitable as pioneers for the prairies. They also introduced the precedent of ethnic and denominational block settlement as a necessary, if not desirable, type of colonization.

The intention of the Dominion Land Act of 1872 was to provide free homesteads measuring a quarter section (i.e., 160 acres or 64.4 hectares) for individual settlers undivided in their political loyalty and culturally assimilable. In the early 1870's, however, the concession of block settlement appeared to be essential for creating a population base on the prairies. Canada used this concession to edge out the United States, with whom it had been competing intensely for the 50,000 Mennonites anxious to leave Russia in 1872.

The first Russian Mennonites who came to Canada were the two most conservative groups (numbering 7,000). The decisive factor in their choice was the American refusal to accede to their request for closed block and village settlement. Their reason for leaving Russia stemmed from the abrogation of religious and cultural privileges granted them by earlier Russian governments, especially exemption from military service and the right to communicate exclusively in German. What attracted them to Canada was less the agricultural potential of the prairie than the prospect of an undisturbed continuation of their way of life within the framework of communal settlement. The settling of the Mennonites in 1874 thus served as a precedent for the formation of not only more Mennonite, but also Hutterite, Roman Catholic, and Doukhobor blocks in western Canada, and it resulted in the creation of a mosaic of sizable ethnic islands in the Anglo-Saxon sea of the Canadian prairies.

The East and West Reserves

The closed area reserved for the Mennonites from Russia was located 35 miles southeast of Winnipeg and was known as the East Reserve. It consisted of twelve townships with 36 sections each. Because the Mennonites were unhappy with the quality of the soil and with the brush and trees covering it, they settled only eight townships. Many chose to settle on the treeless plain west of the Red River. There, in 1876 the West Reserve, comprising seventeen townships, was created, along with a separate small colony of two townships on the Scratching River. In these Reserves the Mennonites rebuilt the communal life they had known in Russia, complete with more than one hundred villages, each laid out in the centuries-old manner along both sides of a single street with provisions for family gardens, a common pasture, a school, a mayor *(Schulze)*, and a minister. Even the building styles -- evident in the efficient joining of the house and barn for greater comfort and protection of humans and animals -- as well as the farming techniques came from their settlements in Russia.

The transfer of the village system facilitated the continuation of their traditionally supportive network of mutual aid and spiritual fellowship and thereby contributed to their eventual farming success. Nevertheless, the Mennonite pioneers faced unprecedented hardships until 1877 and for the purchase of provisions and seed grains they had to draw heavily on a $100,000 federal government loan negotiated in 1875 with Ontario Mennonites as co-signers. Their full repayment of this loan with interest by 1891 indicates their rate of economic success and their serious approach to business matters. Their credit rating was so high that after World War I the CPR was willing to lend them two million dollars for the rescue of their fellow *Russländer* Mennonites.

In its promotion of immigration to the West, the federal government proudly showed off the Mennonite settlements as models for the potential of the unpopulated western wilderness. Governor General of Canada Lord Dufferin, after inspecting the East Reserve in 1877, spoke exuberantly about "so marvelous a transformation" which held great hope and promise for the future. The Mennonite colonies became

model farms, not only because they were economically
successful but also because they were beautifully landscaped
with spectacular flower gardens and specially planned groves
of maple and poplar trees. Prosperity, however, produced
independence, the ultimate dissolution of the villages, and the
continued westward migration of many Manitoba Mennonites.
The strength of their religious convictions has enabled some
of the congregations to preserve their German mother tongue
and cultural identity until the present, but this same strength
also caused severe conflicts with the authorities over the
school question and participation in secular government.

Non-Mennonite rural colonies

From 1890 on, the Mennonite settlements in Manitoba
served as important way stations for Germans intending to
settle in the West. Wealthy Mennonite farmers preferred to
employ German Protestant and Catholic immigrants from
Russia as farmhands. The newcomers thus gained the
opportunity to accumulate funds and experience in Canadian
agriculture. Most German Catholics, however, moved on to
settle in Saskatchewan, while some of the Protestants stayed
to form German Lutheran and Baptist congregations in or
near the East and West Reserves. Lutheran colonies developed, for instance, east of Winnipeg, west of Lake Manitoba,
and along the Saskatchewan border near Langenburg. In 1896,
east of Winnipeg near Beausejour, Brokenhead, and White-
mouth, Germans from Volhynia, joined by coreligionists from
Galicia, Russia, and eastern Germany, began to settle.
Waldersee, west of Lake Manitoba, was founded in 1891 by
Germans from Galicia; in 1896 it received a large influx from
East Prussia, Posen, Volhynia, and the Crimea. Near the
Saskatchewan border, Germans from Volhynia started Fried-
feld in 1913, while in 1900 Germans from Minnesota, South
Russia, Volhynia, Germany, and Romania settled near Inglis
and Grandview.

The significance of Winnipeg

With the opening of the West, Winnipeg rose from a village
of 240 inhabitants in 1871 to be the railway junction, centre of

communications, commercial metropolis and main gateway for immigration to the Canadian prairies. Between 1881 and 1911 nearly 10 percent of its population was of German origin. A growing number of German-speaking migrants heading for the West moved through the city each year. Many sought and found temporary work there to earn the money necessary to start homesteading. Those who worked during the summer months as farmhands near Winnipeg could find work in the city during the winter months. Among its population of 140,000 in 1911-12, Winnipeg counted 12-14,000 residents of German origin.

The growth of Winnipeg's German community and the city's role as a stopover for an increasing number of German-speaking migrants to the West was reflected in the development of secular and church organizations. By 1914, Winnipeg's Germans had fifteen churches (nine of them Lutheran) and four national-origin organizations. These helped German-speaking newcomers procure employment and advised them on the purchase of land. The *Deutsche Vereinigung* was founded in 1884. By 1912 there were also a *Deutsch-Österreich-Ungarischer Verein*, a *Deutsch-Ungarischer Verein*, and a *Deutscher Klub Helvetia*. The oldest German church in Winnipeg was dedicated in 1890 by the Baptists. The Lutheran congregation, in existence since 1888, opened its first church in 1891, and the Catholics built St. Joseph's Church in 1905. The German Oblates serving St. Joseph's Parish had ensured the formation of a homogeneous German Catholic residential neighbourhood around St. Joseph's. They had founded a society that purchased a large suburban sector and sold it piecemeal as building lots to German Catholic immigrants. By 1914 there were seventeen German clergy ministering in the city: eight Lutherans, three Catholics, two of the Evangelical Synod, one Reformed, one Baptist, and one of the Evangelical Association. The German churches maintained six German language schools. In 1889 Canada's most widely read German language newspaper, *Der Nordwesten* (published today as *Kanada Kurier*), and in 1909 Canada's leading Mennonite paper, the *Mennonitische Rundschau*, were launched in Winnipeg.

CHAPTER XIX

ROOTS OF WESTERN CANADA'S GERMAN PIONEERS

    1. The Russian Empire
    2. Romania
    3. The Austro-Hungarian Empire
    4. The United States and Germany

The Russian Empire

Three quarters of the Germans who helped pioneer the opening of the Canadian West had their roots in eastern Europe. Since they arrived as nationals of Russia, Romania, or Austria-Hungary, at times they erroneously labelled themselves as Russians, Romanians, etc. in response to the ethnic origin classification of the Canadian Census. In addition, some were also second- or third-generation emigrants from southwestern Germany while others descended from colonists with a centuries-old presence in eastern Europe. Although all of them had preserved the language, customs, and traditions of their German ancestors, most had lost touch with developments in Germany and had adjusted their lives and ways to conditions in their east European homelands. As loyal subjects of their Russian, Hungarian, or Romanian rulers they felt no allegiance to the modern German state and rejected modern German nationalism. The radical socio-economic changes in 19th-century Germany widened the gulf with backward eastern Europe and increased the differences in attitudes and outlook between ethnic Germans attached to the rural lifestyle of eastern Europe and Germans from the urban and industrial environment of Germany.

More than half of western Canada's pre-World War I German pioneers came directly or indirectly from three regions of the Russian Empire: (1) the Black Sea coast, (2) the Volga, or (3) central, as well as southwestern, Poland, especially Volhynia. In the 1870's Russian push and Canadian pull factors began to coincide to start a migration of German colonists to Canada from these regions. The great liberal reforms of Czar Alexander II in the 1860's which attempted to modernize Russia by abolishing serfdom, introducing equal rights and obligations for all Russian citizens, and terminating various privileges extended to foreigners, must be seen as the main trigger for the rapidly spreading emigration fever. The German colonists on the Volga (240,000 by 1865) and along the Black Sea (150,000 by 1860) had been recruited by Catherine the Great and succeeding czars since the 1760's in order to settle newly conquered South Russia with industrious peasants. They were to bring wealth and progress to backward Russia and, as incentives, were guaranteed exemption from military service, taxes, and government interference in their social and cultural lives. By the 1850's their phenomenal population growth led to their founding daughter colonies all over southern Russia. Their economic success and constant hunger for land had brought one third of South Russia's arable land under their control.

The availability of free land and religious liberty in the Canadian West began to draw emigrants to Canada only when these conditions became restricted in Russia. The first German colonists to leave Russia were Mennonites, who formed a minority among the predominantly Lutheran and Catholic colonies. As separatists and non-resistors they were opposed to any form of military duty. Religious principle was, therefore, their primary reason for leaving Russia. They were followed by others who found it increasingly difficult to acquire land in Russia and by those who experienced discrimination as a result of the growth of Russian nationalism. Once emigration had started for religious reasons in 1874 and a Canadian immigration agency was established in Odessa, a steady stream of emigrants left Russia for all kinds of reasons. The Russian government allowed the German colonists to go but prohibited the emigration of Russians.

Ukrainians did not arrive in Canada until 1891, and Russians not until 1899.

In Volhynia (then part of the Russian Empire), the laws of 1888 and 1892 forbade the sale of land to anyone but native Russian citizens even though German colonists, who had been invited by Polish landlords to lease and cultivate undeveloped lands since the 1830's, numbered 170,000 in 139 villages by 1897. Growing tensions between Russia, Austria-Hungary, and Germany made Volhynia a militarily endangered area. German settlers were suspected of being politically unreliable, and their economic and cultural life was subjected to such increasing restriction that a mass exodus began in the 1890's.

Romania

The relatively large migration of Germans from small Romania to western Canada (mostly to Saskatchewan), amounted to 6 percent of German pre-World War I immigration. It originated in settlements in the Dobrudja. Since the 1840's, these had been populated by German colonists from South Russia. When Romania declared its independence from the Ottoman Empire in 1878 and Dobrudja became a part of Romania, the German colonists were immediately affected by the assertion of Romanian nationalism. Land acquisition by German colonists was severely restricted and in some instances even reversed. After 1890 ethnic Germans were no longer able to buy any land in the Dobrudja. Romanian mayors were imposed on the German villages and universal military service was introduced in 1883. By 1884 the desire to leave Romania appears to have become widespread. In 1885 in Saskatchewan, Baptists arrived from the village of Tulcea and founded Neu Tulcea, later called Edenwold. Entire villages in the Dobrudja, after flourishing briefly, vanished again through emigration. Their German colonists, whose grandparents had left Germany in search of land and freedom first in Russia, then in the Dobrudja, moved on to North America. Some came to Canada directly, others migrated to the northwestern United States and from there to Canada.

The Austro-Hungarian Empire

The Habsburg Empire included Austria, Hungary, Czechoslovakia, most of present-day Yugoslavia and Romania, as well as the former Polish province of Galicia. Eighteen percent of the total pre-World War I German immigration to western Canada came from Austria-Hungary, i.e., predominantly from the non-German parts of the Empire. The largest German exodus took place from Galicia where the German presence dated back to the Middle Ages and the German population numbered 75,000 by 1890. German colonists immigrated to Canada largely from eastern Galicia, which bordered on Volhynia. There, colonists from southwestern Germany had settled among Ukrainians and Poles after the annexation of the province by Austria in 1772. For the Galicia Germans the overpopulation and economic backwardness of the region were aggravated by the consequences of political autonomy, which the imperial government had granted to Galicia. New Polish school laws, polonization of the parishes, restrictions on the purchase of land, and replacement of German government officials by Poles relegated the German colonists, especially the Lutheran ones, to the status of a discriminated minority in their own villages and parishes and drove them into emigration.

The region known as Bukovina supplied a large volume of the first Austrian emigrants to western Canada. All of them settled in Saskatchewan between 1890 and 1900. The Habsburg Emperor had acquired Bukovina (on the southeastern tip of Galicia bordering on Romania) from the Turks in 1775 and intended to rehabilitate it with the help of German farmers from Galicia and the Banat. The Romanian and Ukrainian local authorities and natives of Bukovina, however, did not encourage German colonization on a large scale and the so-called Swabian villages of the colonists never had enough scope to expand. German cultural life was free to develop only in cities like Czernowitz. The emigration fever that seized the Swabian villages of Bukovina spread to their non-German neighbours and made the German colonists the vanguard of Ukrainian and Romanian emigration to Canada.

The last sizable group of Germans from the Habsburg Empire to emigrate to Canada around 1900 were so-called

Danube Swabians from the Banat, a region in southern
Hungary. These Germans had been recruited as colonists in
southwestern Germany after the Austrian defeat of the Turks
in 1716. Due to prosperity and a large natural increase the
German population reached 450,000 by 1900. The difficulty of
obtaining cheap, new farmland was aggravated beginning in
1867 by Hungary's systematic policy of magyarization of
German names, schools, the courts, and government bureau-
cracy. Upward social mobility was closed to those resisting
magyarization. As a result, the educated and entrepreneurial
classes as well as the land-hungry farmers among the Danube
Swabians who wanted to retain their German background saw
emigration as their only future. By 1911, 10 to 20 percent of
Banat Swabians were reported to have left for North America.
The emigration fever also spread to fellow Swabian colonies
in the Batschka and to the Transylvania Saxons, both in
Hungary. From German Austria and today's Czechoslovakia
few Germans went to Canada before 1914.

The United States and Germany

Between 1874 and 1914, another 18 percent of the German
immigration to western Canada consisted of second- or
third-generation German Americans, but only 12 percent
comprised *Reichsdeutsche*.

Among these German Americans, those who descended from
Russian colonists outnumbered the others. As land in the
American Northwest became scarce and expensive, land-
hungry and profit-oriented German Americans were attracted
across the border to Canada by the availability of cheap and
virtually unlimited amounts of fertile virgin land. Many, like
former U.S. Senator Meilicke from Minnesota, came to
engage in mechanized "wheat mining" on a large scale.
Others, like the German-American Catholics who came to
Saskatchewan, hoped to escape denominational and ethnic
assimilation by forming a block settlement in the prairie
wilderness. German-American immigration began in the early
1890's and reached its climax around 1910. Alberta and
Saskatchewan were the preferred destinations.

In spite of the great efforts of the Canadian government, few *Reichsdeutsche* chose Canada as their destination. Throughout the 19th century until 1893, i.e., as long as the mass emigration from Germany lasted, close to 90 percent of *reichsdeutsche* emigrants preferred to settle in the United States. Although the shortest route to the American Midwest led through Canada, only 5 percent of *Reichsdeutsche* transient arrivals during most of the years between 1874 and 1891 stayed in Canada. Numerous factors motivated natives of Germany to choose the American instead of the Canadian West: the existence of a much larger German-speaking community, prior contacts with people in America, more favourable economic and geographic conditions, a higher degree of urbanization, an unfamiliarity with farming on the treeless Canadian prairie, apprehensions about Canada's harsh climate, and fear of ethnic intolerance from the British Canadian host society. In every comparison with America, whose transition from a rural to an industrial society had many parallels in Germany, Canada appeared backward.

CHAPTER XX

GERMANS IN PRE-CONFEDERATION CANADA

1. Settlement in British North America
2. Manifestations of urban community life
3. Cultural contributions

Settlement in British North America

By Confederation in 1867 Canada's population of German origin numbered about 200,000, or nearly 10 percent of the total population of British North America. In Ontario there were 160,000 residents of German origin, in the Maritimes 38,000, and in Quebec 8,000. This meant that Germans comprised 70 percent of Canada's non-British and non-French population.

The pre-Confederation German population was concentrated in two areas: nearly 60 percent lived in or around Ontario's Waterloo County, while 15 percent lived in or near the counties of Lunenburg and Halifax in Nova Scotia. The vast majority of these German Canadians were the descendants of immigrants from southwestern Germany, the United States, and Switzerland. Since the American War of Independence they had migrated to British North America in distinct groups and waves, such as "Hessian" auxiliary troops, United Empire Loyalists, Pennsylvania German Mennonites, Red River colonists, and pioneers in York, Waterloo County, and the Ottawa valley.

Throughout the first half of the 19th century, German settlers were among the pioneer colonizers of large parts of southwestern and eastern Ontario, as well as of the Maritimes.

They were among the first settlers and merchants in British Columbia in the 1850's and among Selkirk's Red River colonists in 1820. Thousands of German Loyalists, many of whom had fought for the British cause in the American War of Independence, helped to create the new provinces of New Brunswick and Upper Canada. By Confederation the German heritage of most of these pioneer settlers was disappearing because their second or third generation of descendants in the Maritimes, the Niagara district, along the St. Lawrence and the Bay of Quinte, and in York (Toronto) assimilated into the rapidly growing anglophone or francophone populations. The original German character of pioneer settlements was preserved only in areas with a continued influx of German-speaking immigrants, such as Waterloo County, or where the settlers owed their first allegiance to their inherited church and considered the German language and culture an integral part of their religious creed, as among Mennonites, Amish, Tunkers, and Moravians.

Manifestations of urban community life

By the 1860's most of the major Canadian cities, such as Montreal, Toronto, Hamilton, Berlin (Kitchener), Ottawa, and Halifax had German communities. The appearance of urban German life can be traced to the beginning of the mid-19th century spectacular growth of Canadian cities. In 1846 twenty German families were counted in Toronto's population of some 20,000. Among them were Abraham and Samuel Nordheimer. They had emigrated from Bamberg to New York in 1839 and from there to Toronto where they opened a music business in 1844. Toronto's burgeoning urban development attracted a German community of nearly 1,000 by 1871, mostly craftsmen and businessmen who contributed notably to the city's economy. The most prominent German entrepreneur was Berlin-born Theodor August Heintzman, who immigrated from Buffalo (New York) in 1860. He was the founder of Canada's manufacturing industry of musical instruments; German entrepreneurs remained leaders in this industry until 1914. His son-in-law was a co-founder of Toronto's first church for Lutherans in 1851.

In Hamilton, the next largest commercial centre in Ontario and the major thoroughfare for immigrants from Quebec, Montreal and New York, 2,000 Germans were reported to have been looking for work as early as 1852. From 1851 to 1856, while the city's population grew from 10,300 to 27,500, German immigrants found work in such German-owned enterprises as Richard Mott Wanzer's sewing machine factory, founded in 1860. Rifles and guns were manufactured by Heinrich Kretschmann and Julius Winckler. German Lutherans organized their first church, St. Paul's, in 1858, and German Catholics published a weekly bulletin. German Methodists built their first church in Canada in Hamilton in 1861. German secular life was reflected in the advertisements of German associations and the cultural events they sponsored. In February 1860 the *Hamilton Spectator* reported on the first German masquerade ball attended by more than one hundred persons. The organizer was the German *Eintracht* Society, and the German lawyer and North German Lloyd representative Wilhelm Herrman served as chairman. Hamilton was a focal point of German cultural activity in Canada by the time of Confederation as is evidenced by the launching in 1861 of a "German Theatre" by a Mr. Pelzer, the first anatomical museum by the German physician Dr. Emil Querner, as well as of a German Benevolent Society in 1863. In addition, two German-language papers were published in the 1860's and a German by the name of Ahrens was police chief in 1865. By 1871, 1,300 residents of German origin were counted in Hamilton.

A Canadian of Swiss-German descent, Louis Gugy, was Montreal's chief of police in 1835 when he was elected the first president of the very first German Benevolent Society in Canada, the *Deutsche Gesellschaft zu Montreal.* His deputy and successor was physician Peter Arnoldi, son of a prominent German immigrant in Quebec. The backgrounds of the Society's 76 charter members -- mostly merchants, butchers, innkeepers, and artisans -- reflect the heterogeneous nature of Montreal's early German community. Only 19 were natives of Germany (15 of them from Württemberg). Half were Canadian-born, of whom 25 descended from Germany, and 10 were non-Germans married to German wives. Four were natives of Switzerland, 4 of France, 4 of the United States, 6 of England, and 1 of Scotland. Assisting needy immigrants was the main purpose of the Society. Needless to say, the mass migrations of the following decades afforded ample opportunities for this. Members of the *Deutsche Gesellschaft* together with new immigrants organized St. John's Lutheran Church in 1853 and in 1857 laid the foundation for the singing clubs *Germania* and *Eintracht*. Between 1842, 1850, and 1871 Montreal's German population increased from 207 (including 176 Canadian-born) to 317 and 1,345, while the city's population grew from 48,000 (in 1850) to 131,000.

In the 1850's one of Canada's best known and most successful businessmen and urban developers of German descent was Samuel Zimmerman. Born humbly in Pennsylvania in 1815, he rose to fame and fortune as a contractor for the Welland Canal in the 1840's and the Niagara Falls Suspension Bridge completed in 1855. The latter had been designed by the eminent German-American engineer Johann August Roebling. Zimmerman owned hotels, steamers, banks, railways, and some 18,000 acres of real estate, especially in Toronto and Hamilton. When a railway accident ended his life in 1857 he had become the chief railway promoter and contractor for the Great Western and five other Canadian railways. The town of Niagara Falls owes much of its rapid development after 1848 to the initiatives of Zimmerman who was its largest property owner and promoter. As famed for his generous public and private gifts as for his diligence to ensure the success of his projects, he was believed to have been the richest man in Canada. He was on intimate terms with leading politicians and his sway over other men "virtually made him ruler of the province for several years," according to his biographers.

Cultural contributions

German Canadians in the first half of the 19th century pioneered not only the cultivation and settlement of large tracts of wilderness land in eastern Canada, but were also cultural pioneers in this formative period of Canadian history. In many areas of Ontario and the Maritimes they founded the first churches, organized the first German schools, and launched the first (German-language) newspapers. These institutions often remained for some time the only ones far and wide. By 1850 German-language denominational schools were so widespread in Ontario that the School Act of the early 1850's legitimized German as a language of instruction in districts where Germans represented the majority of the taxpayers. Between 1835 and 1867, eighteen different German-language papers were published in southwestern Ontario.

German musicians like Friedrich Glackemeyer, Franz Vogler, Theodor F. Molt, and Johann Christoph Brauneis left a deep imprint on Canadian music. German music teachers, band leaders, singing clubs, conductors, composers, or instrument makers frequently brought the first music to a locality. There was at least one of them in almost every large community that contained German immigrants. In 1866 conductor Prof. Charles F. Müller's Hamilton "Cecilian Glee Club" was the first Canadian participant at the American *Sängerfest* celebrated since 1849 in Erie, Pennsylvania. Music historian Helmut Kallmann refers to the first half of the 19th century as the "German period" in Canadian music history. Similarly, the paintings and drawings of such outstanding contemporary German and Swiss German-born artists as Peter Rindisbacher, William von Moll Berczy, Cornelius David Krieghoff, and Otto Jacobi have become a treasured national heritage. They were unsurpassed in their time and caused some critics to characterize the years 1800-1870 a "German-Canadian period" in Canadian art history.

German pioneer physicians, especially several who came with the German auxiliary troops in the 1780's, are renowned for their significant contributions. Some of them, such as Daniel Arnoldi, Heinrich Loedel, Friedrich Wilhelm Oliva and Anthony von Iffland, organized medical training and promoted medical care and medical science in Quebec and Ontario.

In early- and mid-19th century Quebec, Canadians of German descent served as top government officials, administrators, and lawyers. They were also found among the ringleaders of the Quebec rebellion of 1837.

CHAPTER XXI

DESTINATION OTTAWA VALLEY

1. Opening up the Ottawa-Huron Tract
2. Recruiting German immigrants
3. German settlements
4. Cultural and linguistic retention

Opening up the Huron-Ottawa Tract

The settlement of 12,000 Germans in the Ottawa Valley between 1857 and 1887 may be considered the fruit of the Canadian government's first systematic attempt in the 19th century to recruit immigrants in Germany. By the mid-1850's the Province of Canada, with a widely dispersed population of slightly more than two million, witnessed an unprecedented mass migration of Germans moving through to Michigan and the American Midwest. Many German immigrants heading for the American frontier from the ports of Quebec, Montreal, or New York, preferred the relatively short and cheap route through southwestern Ontario. While few of these migrants stayed in Canada, their migratory movement attracted many Canadian settlers to join them. The Canadian government became alarmed by the momentum of the American westward flow, fearing the emigration of Canadians and loss of Canadian control over the uninhabited border regions. It wanted to attract a permanent population into the strategically important Huron-Ottawa Tract and to create a viable lumbering and agricultural industry in the region between the lower Ottawa River and Georgian Bay. Efforts to divert for this purpose a share of the German mass migration to America form the background to the story of German settlement in the Ottawa valley.

To provide access for settlers, the government decided to build through the wilderness from the Ottawa River to Georgian Bay between 1851 and 1856 three colonization roads called the Opeongo, Hastings, and Addington Roads. Along these roads free grants of land were offered to settlers. Of significance to settlers was the position of the uncompleted Opeongo Road. It was the only road that could be reached from the Ottawa River at the road's starting point near Pembroke. The government ignored the fact that the land along the Road was of marginal agricultural value. Since the free homestead ground was located on the fringe of the Canadian shield, much of it was stony and infertile. Nevertheless, the Opeongo Road was the one that attracted substantial numbers of German settlers. The advantages of settlement along the Road were first advertised unsuccessfully in Britain in 1856; nonetheless, the first settlers in the district were 500 Canadian residents of Irish, British, and French-Canadian origin. Their background is still reflected in the predominantly English place names of Renfrew County. Although German immigrants from southwestern Germany may have been employed as construction workers, loggers, and farmhands in the area as early as 1855, the first documented German settlers in Renfrew County appeared in 1857. By 1860 the German population in the county was 900. By 1870 it is estimated to have risen to 5,000 and by 1891 to 13,000. Although immigration continued until the 1880's, much of the population growth after the 1870's was due to natural increase.

Recruiting German immigrants

The influx of German settlers into the upper Ottawa valley north of the Opeongo Road in Renfrew County and across the River into the adjoining counties of Quebec, was rather substantial in view of the marginal quality of the land. This influx may be attributed to four factors: first, the activities of German-speaking immigration agents in combination with a systematic advertising campaign in Germany; second, the unprecedented mass exodus from Germany of people in search of free or cheap land; third, the American Civil War; and finally, the overflow of German settlers from Waterloo County.

Between 1855 and 1866 as many as six Canadian immigration agents of German origin were at work directing emigrants from Germany to the Ottawa valley. Three of them -- William Sinn, William Wagner and M. Bechel -- travelled through Prussia. They diligently promoted Canada among local German administrators, clergymen, innkeepers, and merchants by lecturing and distributing literature. Other German-speaking agents, stationed at the Quebec and Ottawa ports, guided the arriving immigrants to another agent in Pembroke or at the Opeongo Road. In the advertisements and promotional literature, which, since 1857, were distributed in large quantities in Germany, the advantages of settling in the Ottawa valley were painted in the rosiest colours, while the drawbacks were deliberately played down or passed over.

Since similar promotional efforts in the British Isles and Norway did not result in a comparable emigration from these countries, the German influx into the Ottawa valley must have been conditioned by other factors as well. One of these was the peaking of the mass exodus from Germany to America (1852-1873), which also increased the flow of German immigration to Canada substantially. The German movement into the Ottawa Valley was further accelerated by the instability wrought by the American Civil War, but it was certainly also attributable to the fact that from the 1860's, for the first time, a large number of people began to emigrate from northeastern Germany.

From the 18th century until the mid-1850's southwestern Germany had been the main source area of emigrants from Germany, most of whom had contacts with friends and relatives already living in the United States. The new emigrants from Prussia and Mecklenburg, mostly working-class people and agricultural labourers of German, Polish (Kashub), and Wendish origin, lacked contacts in North America and could be won over with the promise of free land. In the early 1860's Canadian immigration agents, especially William Wagner, were aware of the promising prospects of recruiting emigrants from these parts of Germany. From the late 1850's, these agents also directed land-hungry German-Canadian settlers from Waterloo County, where immigration and natural increase caused a shortage of cheap land, to the Ottawa district.

German settlements

Germans formed the predominant group of pioneer settlers in 15 townships in the upper Ottawa valley; eleven of these were in Renfrew County (Ontario), and one each was in the Ontario counties of Frontenac, Lennox and Addington and the Quebec counties of Pontiac and Labelle. In the entire district 15 small places and post offices (such as Augsburg, Woermke, Rosenthal, Kramer, and Hoffman) and 22 lakes, creeks, and points were named by its German settlers. In the larger towns such as Pembroke, Germans formed a minority. The more prominent place names are English and reflect the fact that British pioneers occupied the best land before German settlers arrived. In Bowman Township (Labelle County), where land was 40 percent cheaper than in Renfrew County, the first 200-300 German settlers arrived in 1861. They are reported to have come with considerable means and probably would have migrated to the American Midwest had the Civil War not broken out.

Although logging was a major industry in the area, the German settlers concentrated on farming. They had emigrated in order to own land and to farm. Since removing the forest was arduous toil for which the German immigrants were not prepared, if they could afford to do so, they preferred to buy land that others had cleared. But even then they discovered, to their disappointment, that a recurrent harvest of stones awaited them and their children. For removing stumps and large rocks the German pioneers ingeniously devised stump pullers and stone-lifting machines. They quickly acquired a reputation for being able to adjust where settlers of other nationalities failed to make a living. "They do not follow other pursuits such as lumbering and milling," one government official tried to explain their success, "but devote their whole time to their farms and keep out of debt." The mutual aid and hospitality of a community of fellow countrymen no doubt helped adaptation to the difficult environment.

Itinerant Lutheran clergymen of the American Pittsburgh Synod enabled the formation of congregations as early as 1861. The regular church services and schools they established in the German language can be credited with keeping German ethnicity in the Ottawa valley alive until the 1970's. "As indisputable proof of their industry and frugality," the above-quoted government report of 1887 pointed out, "the Germans in these townships maintain their own schools, in which is taught English during one half of the day and German in the other half." Present-day Ladysmith (Pontiac County) was founded by the Bretzlaffs from Prussia in 1868. The German parochial school started upon their arrival lasted for a century, and was the only school in the district until the establishment of an English school in Thorne Township in 1885. German is still spoken in its Lutheran congregation (founded in 1872) and among some of the descendants of its first pioneers. Pastor Christiansen of Arnprior even launched a German-language weekly for the area, the *Deutsche Post,* which lasted from 1901 until 1916. Today 20 percent of the population of Renfrew County claim German ethnic origin, and many artifacts attest to the German heritage in the Ottawa valley.

CHAPTER XXII

LITTLE GERMANY IN WATERLOO COUNTY

1. German life in Waterloo County until
   Confederation
2. The settlement of Waterloo County
3. The origins of Kitchener-Berlin

German life in Waterloo County

Waterloo County and its capital of Berlin (now called Kitchener) stand out today as the centre of German-Canadian culture. In 19th-century Canada this area was known as New Germany. Here, settlers of German origin and their German heritage were dominant from the beginning of settlement until 1916. Until the eve of World War II residents of Kitchener referred to Waterloo County as *Deutschländle* (Little Germany). By the 1860's three decades of steady immigration from Germany had transplanted many features of urban culture from Germany to Waterloo County. Two of these were the German choir and the *Turnverein* which could be found in all the major towns of Waterloo County. Besides singing and gymnastics, they promoted fellowship and German patriotic sentiments. Several county towns had their own German-language theatre and newspaper. In the 1860's choral societies evolved into German secular clubs, which took on broader social functions. In Waterloo and Berlin they organized concerts, dances, parades, reunions, and picnics, as well as educational, cultural, and charitable projects. The first Canadian *Sängerfest* was a three-day festivity held in Berlin in August 1862 with choirs from as far away as Toronto, Buffalo, and Detroit attending. The 1863 *Sängerfest* was held in Waterloo. Events such as the *Friedensfest* and the annual

Sängerfeste became highlights of German-Canadian cultural life. The *Friedensfest* of 1871 on the occasion of Germany's unification and victory over France was celebrated by more than 10,000 people in Berlin, Ontario, including the city's English-speaking citizens who conveyed "heartfelt" and "genuine esteem" to their German fellow citizens.

In the Waterloo county seat of Berlin, English Canadians recognized German Canadians as the charter group until World War I. In numerous addresses Canadian governors, officials, and visitors of all kinds paid homage to the German character and virtues and encouraged the community leaders to maintain Berlin's German identity within the dominant Anglo-Saxon culture of Canada. Berlin's first leaders were recent German immigrants who had become successful businessmen and merchants. Arriving with little more than their skills as artisans and craftsmen and a determination to succeed, twenty-seven had managed to establish flourishing industrial firms between 1852 and 1870. These firms employed seven hundred German newcomers, thus helping to increase Berlin's population from less than 1,000 in 1854 to nearly 3,000 in 1871. Prominent were E. Vogelsang's button factory, the Boehmer Box Company, Louis Breithaupt's tannery, Wilhelm Hespeler's distillery (now Seagram's), J.M. Schneider's sausage factory, and A.L. Breithaupt and Louis Weber's rubber company (now Uniroyal), to name a few. Another successful leader was Hugo Krantz, who opened a general store upon his arrival in 1855, advanced to town clerk within three years, to mayor of Berlin within ten years, and to Member of Parliament within 22 years.

Berlin's prosperous businessmen were role models for the German newcomers who shared a common social background with them and kept them in power. The unique equality of opportunity prevailing in Berlin was reinforced by the absence of a local Anglo-Saxon social and economic elite, typically superimposed on other immigrant communities in Canada. The community adhered to a high work ethic and strict social mores. Unemployment, crime, prostitution, and social tensions were rarely evident. Accordingly, Berlin was spared the class and racial strife, labour unrest, slums, and sectarianism that characterized urban growth in other parts of Canada.

This endurance of a strong sense of community has been noted by all outside observers and historians.

The settlement of Waterloo County

Waterloo County consists of five townships of which two, Waterloo and Woolwich townships, had been opened up and settled by Pennsylvania German Mennonites since the beginning of the century. They had bought 60,000 acres of the so-called German Company Land on the Grand River from a real estate broker in 1800, who in turn had bought it from the Indians in 1798. By the 1820's, the Mennonites formed sizable minorities in the adjoining townships of Wellesley and North Dumphries. The latter had originally been developed by Scots. In Wilmot Township, Amish Mennonites under Bavarian-born Christian Nafziger acquired their first large tract of land. First-generation immigrants, they arrived from Germany via Pennsylvania in 1823. From Wilmot, the Amish spread to other parts of Ontario. The trek of the Mennonite Conestogas from Pennsylvania ended in the late 1820's. By that time the Mennonites, who were mainly interested in individual homesteading, had founded no more than a few hamlets such as Ebytown, Waterloo, and Preston in Waterloo Township and Conestogo, St. Jacobs, and Elmira in Woolwich Township.

The end of Mennonite treks coincided with the onset of mass migrations from southwest Germany that brought many German artisans and craftsmen to the area en route to the American West. The Mennonites needed farmhands and appreciated the skills of the immigrants. As neighbours they preferred Germans to Anglo-Saxons. The closeness of the immigrants' southwest German dialect to the Pennsylvania Dutch accent made them feel at home in Waterloo. The large influx from Germany continued for three decades and transformed Waterloo and adjoining counties dramatically. Their crafts and trades supplied the needs of an ever-growing market. Since the needs of the Mennonite farms in Waterloo and Woolwich townships were limited, the new immigrants began to move into Wilmot and Wellesley townships. In 1853, when Waterloo County's present geographical form was determined, German-speaking settlers were predominant in four of its five townships. Strasburg, Freiburg, Heidelberg, Baden, Mannheim, and Bamberg are among the many German names pointing to the origin of these settlers. German Lutherans and Catholics settled side by side with Mennonites. In the 1850's German-language newspapers were published in four Waterloo County towns. By then the still predominantly agricultural county was unable to absorb more immigrants and German newcomers along with Waterloo settlers moved on to Bruce and Grey counties, to the Huron Tract, and to the Ottawa Valley.

The origins of Kitchener-Berlin

In 1852 Berlin was no more than a village of 800 inhabitants. Nearby Galt was economically and politically more significant, and even Preston had better communications, more industries, and a larger German population. Nevertheless, Berlin grew to become the capital of German-Canadian culture in three stages, from Mennonite hamlet to flourishing market centre for German immigrants and, finally, in 1852 to county seat, which was its most important turning point. As the administrative capital of Waterloo County, it rose almost inevitably during this time of continued German immigration to become the social and religious centre of the region and after its connection to the Grand Trunk Railway in 1856, also the economic hub.

The selection of Berlin as county seat must be largely attributed to the stubborn and persistent lobby of its ambitious citizens. One of them, Heinrich Petersen, brought a printing press by oxen from Pennsylvania in 1835 and launched Canada's first German-language newspaper, the *Canada Museum und Allgemeine Zeitung.* It was succeeded in 1841 by *Der Deutsche Canadier.* This paper established Berlin's role as the centre of Canada's German population and pressed Berlin's claim to be the district town. To strengthen its claim, the issue of July 27, 1837, suggested the construction of fourteen new houses and the gathering of all kinds of workers in the locality, such as a "potter, chair and spinning-wheel maker, bookbinder, printer, windmill maker, saddler, shoemaker, smith, carpenter, pumpmaker, beer brewer, hotelman, dry goods and grocery stores, weaver, tailor, mason, wagon maker, clockmaker and some day labourers." The German craftsmen were eager to apply their expertise and market their skills. One progressive businessman, furniture maker John Hoffmann, surprised Galt and Guelph businessmen in 1846 with the first use of steam power in the region.

To appreciate the ambition of these Germans one must realize that Berlin received its name only in 1833, two years before the *Canada Museum* was launched. The name was introduced by the Mennonite pioneer of the area, Bishop Eby, as an appropriate designation for the hamlet the first few German immigrants had established near his meeting house. Before the arrival of these Germans, only a Mennonite saddlery, blacksmith, and carpenter shop as well as a roadhouse had existed near Bishop Eby's meeting house on the site known as Ebytown. Located in the midst of a dense forest, it consisted in 1833 of a few workshops, the two stores and twenty-five dwellings -- mostly log buildings.

A letter from Philipp Lautenschlager, an emigrant from Herchenrode to Waterloo Township in 1831, to his family in Germany, explains what attracted the first German immigrants to Waterloo. Not only was there "money to be earned as easily as making hay, if one was willing to work," he wrote. Lautenschlager was equally impressed with the low price of land and with the general advantageous lifestyle: the people wore good clothes, they ate meat and butter three times a day, no one needed to do much walking because they could ride horseback or in a buggy, women had no need to work in the barn or in the fields, no one needed to fear war, and everyone was free. Eby sold land to many immigrants from Germany and promoted the *Canada Museum.* He and other Mennonites played a prominent role in the development of Berlin and its environment. The origins of Kitchener may thus be traced to the interaction and cooperation of Pennsylvania German Mennonites with immigrants from Germany, as these two German-speaking pioneer groups pursued the challenges and opportunities offered by the development of Upper Canada.

CHAPTER XXIII

FIRST MASS EXODUS FROM GERMANY TO
CANADA

1. Immigration from Germany, 1790-1867
2. Settlement in the Niagara Peninsula and the
    Huron Tract
3. Abortive colonization at the Red River and in
    York
4. Causes of the exodus from Germany

Immigration from Germany, 1790-1867

The German-speaking immigrants who settled in Canada
between the end of the American War of Independence and
Canadian Confederation fall into four major groups -- the
Pennsylvania German Mennonites, the United Empire Loyalists, the "Hessians," and those who came from the European
continent after the Napoleonic Wars. The last group,
estimated to be around 50,000, formed the largest and most
enduring element. Many of them settled in such areas as
Waterloo County and the Niagara Peninsula, which had been
opened up earlier by one of the abovementioned groups of
German-speaking pioneers. Others became pioneers in the
Upper Canadian wilderness, for example, in the Huron Tract
and the Ottawa Valley. A few took part in such colonization
failures as Selkirk's Red River and Moll-Berczy's York
(Toronto) colonies. From the 1850's, natives of Germany were
drawn to rapidly growing Canadian cities where they formed
the first German-Canadian urban communities.

Canada has always been eclipsed by the United States among
continental Europeans bound for North America. In the first
half of the 19th century, few Germans left Europe in order to

migrate to Canada. Canada was virtually unknown and considered less attractive, while the advantages of America were well advertised, often by friends and relatives who had migrated there earlier. Until 1846, when sailing ships from Hamburg and Bremen took emigrants directly to Quebec for the first time, virtually no Germans had arrived from Europe in Canadian ocean ports. This route became patronized largely by impoverished emigrants because the small and overcrowded ships sailing it offered lower rates. It reached the peak of its popularity among Germans when record numbers of people left Germany in the 1850's. Of the over 40,000 Germans landing in Quebec during 1850-1857, however, three quarters moved on to the American West. Ten to twelve thousand remained in Canada, partly because they were too poor to continue their journey to the American West and partly because the government appointed a German-speaking agent in Quebec who tried to direct the immigrants to Canadian destinations.

The vast majority of pre-Confederation Canada's German-speaking immigrants from continental Europe entered Canada by way of an American seaport, even after the direct shipping connection to Quebec had been opened. They did not come to North America in order to settle in Canada, but became Canadians more or less by accident while travelling through Canada en route to the American frontier. Throughout the first half of the 19th century the main route to the American West went from New York, Boston, Baltimore, or Philadelphia across Lake Ontario and the Niagara River through southwestern Ontario. Historian Mabel Dunham relates how the Mennonite farmers travelling between Waterloo and Niagara "always found a corner in their conestogas for pedestrians who might be going their direction, and they took many a German not only across the river but as far into Upper Canada as they cared to go, to Waterloo, or to Woolwich." Natives of Germany who had immigrated to the United States and who originally intended only to travel through Canada to the American West thus formed the bulk of Canada's first permanent German immigrants. At the same time most of the immigrants from Germany who disembarked in Canadian ports moved on to America.

Settlement in the Niagara Peninsula and the Huron Tract

Between the 1830's and 1860's, the Niagara district became the second most favoured destination--after Waterloo County -- for immigrants from Germany. Scattered villages of Mennonite farmers and Loyalist pioneers of German origin were already in the area. The employment opportunities and German-speaking neighbourhood these Mennonites and Loyalists offered to German immigrants on their way to the West induced some of them to remain in the Niagara Peninsula. One of the first settlements of the new immigrants was New Germany (also known as Black Creek and now called Snyder) in Willoughby Township, Welland County. It was settled between 1825 and 1835 by groups of people from southwest Germany and Alsace. They came via New York, proceeding tediously in flat-bottom boats, drawn by horses and oxen, through the Barge Canal to Buffalo. There they crossed the Niagara River into Canada. New Germany, although just across the border from bustling Buffalo, was carved out of the wilderness by them. When its Lutheran pioneers organized St. John's congregation, the parishioners had to travel on almost impassable log roads and dangerous trails through dense forests to attend service every four weeks in some settler's log cabin.

In 1847 Rainham, Stonybridge, New Germany (Black Creek), and Jordan were known as small German settlements, and Clinton, Louth, St. Catherines, and Niagara were heavily populated with Germans. Until the 1860's, successive groups of immigrants from Germany continued to settle in townships with large German communities. The 1871 Census showed one quarter of the Niagara Peninsula's population of 80,000 to be of German origin. After 1870, German immigration into the area ceased and after 1890 the use of the German language declined. Rapid assimilation was aided by the continuing immigration of non-German residents, which compelled German Catholic congregations to merge with Irish Catholic parishes and German Lutherans to join English Methodists and Presbyterians. Today, few remember the Niagara Peninsula's original German heritage.

Immigrants from Germany took a prominent part in the opening of the Huron Tract, a huge virgin forest a million

acres in size to the north and west of Waterloo County. In
1829, Sebastian Freyvogel, a German Swiss who had migrated
to Pennsylvania in 1806, and from there to Waterloo in 1827,
became the first settler in Perth County. On the road cut by
the Canada Land Company across the virgin forest to Lake
Huron in 1828, he erected an inn that became the nucleus of
the German settlement of Sebastopol. In the 1830's and
1840's virtually all of South Easthope Township was developed by Germans who organized the first school in the district
in 1842. In 1829, Bavarian-born Andreas Seebach became the
first settler of Ellice Township; his homestead near Sebring-
ville became known as Seebach's Hill. In the vicinity, pioneers
from Germany settled in Rostock, Wartburg, Kuhryville, and
Brunner. The southern townships of Bruce and Grey counties
were settled predominantly by German immigrants who came
by way of nearby Waterloo County. There, lack of opportunities produced a reservoir of colonists for Perth, Huron, Bruce,
and Grey counties. The launching of seven German-language
newspapers between 1863 and 1870 attests to the cultural
vitality of the German communities in the Huron Tract.

Abortive colonization at the Red River and in York

   Except for the Lunenburg settlement of 1750, the two
earliest colonization attempts involving German-speaking
immigrants from Europe were a failure. In 1823, ten
German-Swiss families led by Christian Hay became the first
German-speaking pioneers in Huron County, where they
founded the settlements of Bern and Zurich in Hay Township.
They were among the disillusioned settlers who had abandoned Selkirk's Red River colony two years after their arrival
in 1821.

   The Red River colony at today's site of Winnipeg had been
planned as an ambitious agricultural venture by the Scottish
nobleman Lord T.D. Selkirk who had bought a controlling
interest in the Hudson's Bay Company. Selkirk desired to help
displaced, poverty-stricken Scottish tenants and strengthen his
company's control over the remote Red River cross roads
against the incursions of its rival, the North-West Company.
For the protection of the first 300 Scots who settled in Red

River in 1817, one hundred German and Swiss-German soldiers from the disbanded de Meuron and de Wattewil regiments were stationed nearby at so-called "German Creek" (now Seine River). In honour of the patron saint of the Germans, the entire colony was named St. Boniface. In order to persuade the soldiers to stay and settle, another 200 colonists, including brides for the soldiers, were recruited in Switzerland and Alsace. Enduring great privations, they reached the colony in 1821 by way of Hudson Bay, only to realize they had been lured by deception. Instead of the promised arrangements for successful farming, they found themselves in virgin bushland hundreds of miles from civilization without adequate supplies, roads, markets, or protection from floods, grasshoppers, and the severe climate. The first colonists left in 1822 for La Pointe (in what became Minnesota) and the remaining 250 German-speaking families and soldiers followed them by 1826. One of the colonists was the Swiss-German artist Peter Rindisbacher whose watercolour paintings depicting frontier life at the Red River are acclaimed as "the earliest pictoral record of the country west of the Great Lakes."

In a similar abortive colonization venture some thirty years earlier, Governor Simcoe of Upper Canada offered Markham Township, a wilderness of 60,000 acres 30 kilometers north of Toronto, to an artist-teacher-land speculator of many talents, a certain William Moll-Berczy from Wallerstein, Germany, for development and resale to new settlers. In 1794 Berczy brought to Markham 190 settlers whom he had recruited in Germany for a similar project in New York that turned out to be unfeasible. In return for committing themselves to Berczy for six years, each settler was to receive a 200-acre lot in freehold. The project was well funded by a group of New York investors and speculators who called themselves the German Company. In order to reach Markham, Berczy's contract called for the construction of a road through the virgin forest from Lake Ontario to Lake Simcoe. This road eventually became Toronto's Yonge Street. Within three years the settlers cleared one quarter of the land, cultivated fields and built a model settlement whose "German Mills" became known in the entire province. But unrest among Berczy's settlers and frictions with his American investors led to the undoing of the project. The government rescinded Berczy's grant in 1797 for allegedly defaulting on some of the terms of his contract, and the colony disbanded in bankruptcy. Today Moll-Berczy is honoured as the co-founder of Toronto and the architect of Toronto's first public buildings, which he designed while appealing the cancellation of his grant.

Causes of the exodus from Germany

German emigration to North America reaches back to the beginnings of the European colonization of the New World. From the 17th to the mid-19th century most of the German migrants came from southwestern Germany. When peace returned to Europe in 1815 after the long period of French revolutionary and Napoleonic Wars, the southwest German migration to America increasingly assumed epidemic-like proportions. In order to explain the causes of this mass exodus, migration researchers distinguish between push and pull factors, i.e., on the one hand, conditions that compel emigrants to leave their homelands and, on the other hand, the attractions that induce them to migrate to a certain country. The reasons people emigrated from Germany in the 19th century were almost exclusively economic and social, while in previous centuries wars, political oppression, and the desire for religious freedom had been major causes of emigration. The legacy of dislocations and upheavals caused by the Napoleonic Wars was reinforced by the fundamental changes wrought by the English Industrial Revolution and felt by the ordinary people in Britain and on the European continent.

Between 1815 and 1855 Germany suffered from acute economic backwardness, overpopulation, and pauperism. These were the chief push factors. The growth of modern, steam-powered industry in Britain and France made agrarian Germany a backward country until it, too, became industrial-ized in the second half of the 19th century. The importation of cheap English industrial products, such as linen and clothes, put many traditional German tradesmen and crafts-men out of business; unemployment and poverty were widespread. The situation was aggravated by an unprecedented population explosion and a revolution of rising expectations. Until the 1860's the German economy was unable to provide work for the growing number of unemployed, economically ruined, and starving Germans. Overpopulation and poverty were particularly severe in southwestern Germany, where small-scale agriculture and wine growing formed the mainstays of life. In this region a growing number of citizens and, in fact, entire communities came to depend for their survival on community and state welfare. Emigrants from these states remember their fatherland as the *Hungerland.*

As the misery in Germany increased, so also grew the appeal of the free, independent, and prosperous republic of the United States of America. The chief attractions of Canada, if it was known at all, were the cheap passages to Quebec after 1847 and the advertisement that Buffalo and the American Midwest could be reached faster from there. In order to reduce the overwhelming mass poverty, the rulers of the southwestern German states at first tolerated emigration (in the 18th century it was prohibited), then encouraged it, and finally assisted in the transport of needy and socially undesirable individuals to North America. Between 1847 and 1855 the governments of Baden, Württemberg, and Hessen even dissolved entire impoverished communities and shipped their inhabitants at state expense to Quebec and Saint John, N.B., until protests from North America stopped these practices. Most Germans, however, despairing of the future for themselves and their children, went voluntarily and with their own resources: 1.7 million to the U.S.A. and 62,000 to Canada from 1820-1869.

CHAPTER XXIV

THE PENNSYLVANIA-GERMAN MENNONITE MIGRATIONS

1. Settlement in Ontario
2. The Mennonites in America
3. Origins of the Mennonites

Settlement in Ontario

The term Mennonites, synonymous with Anabaptists, refers to all those radical Protestant groups descending from the 16th-century German and Dutch Reformation that do not recognize any external religious and civil authority in matters of conscience and faith. They reject the official Protestant and Catholic state churches and want to live every aspect of their lives according to the teachings of the Gospel. Among their central beliefs are nonresistance, adult (believers') baptism, and a communal life of discipleship. Separating themselves from governments and the surrounding society, from Catholics and other Protestants, and often even from each other on account of reinterpretations of their faith, these "separatists" look back on a history of persecution and martyrdom. For almost 500 years they have migrated far and wide in search of homelands that would offer them liberty, security, and prosperity. In North America the first German Mennonites settled in Pennsylvania in 1683 at the invitation of William Penn. As soon as the frontier in Upper Canada was opened up in the 1780's and the British colonial authorities offered an abundance of good land, along with religious freedom and the prospect of cultural autonomy, the Mennonites began to advance into Canada.

The American rebellion against the British was a catalyst,

but not the sole impetus, for the Mennonite migrations to Canada, which began in 1786. The Mennonites distrusted the new American experiment in government, the fervour of American nationalism and the turmoil following the War of Independence. Their sympathies tended to lie with the Crown, which had guaranteed their religious freedom. Population pressure was another reason for the migration. In Pennsylvania the good land had all been occupied and it became difficult for Mennonite farmers to provide a farm for every son. The Mennonites looked for new homes in Upper Canada rather than in Ohio because the former was easier to reach: there were several river routes and fewer mountain barriers. Since cheap land was plentiful in Canada and serious settlers were officially solicited, the Mennonites were attracted by the prospect of acquiring large blocks of land where they could preserve their distinct German cultural and social life. The free land in Canada granted to thousands of German soldiers (Loyalists and "Hessians") who had defended the Crown, as well the German names given to the four districts of Upper Canada -- Lunenburg, Mecklenburg, Nassau and Hesse -- to flatter the Hannoverian King of England, gave rise to the hope that the Mennonites' German culture could be better maintained in Canada than in revolutionary America's melting pot.

Unlike the Loyalists, Mennonites did not qualify for free land grants despite their Loyalist sympathies. They bought land the Loyalists wanted to sell in Lincoln, Welland, Waterloo, and York. The first parties from Lancaster and adjoining counties in Pennsylvania took up land just across the Niagara border at "the Twenty" and near Fort Erie between 1786 and 1788. The Waterloo settlement was started by Mennonites from Franklin County, Pennsylvania, who wintered at "the Twenty" in 1799 and then followed the Indian Trail to Brantfort. From a speculator named Richard Beasley they acquired land on the Grand River although that land had been granted to Loyalist Indians. By 1802, 25 Mennonite families had already arrived in Waterloo, and more were on their way from different parts of Pennsylvania, when it was discovered that Beasley's lands were mortgaged. In order to get title to the land, Mennonites were asked to buy the entire block of 60,000 acres for 10,000 dollars, a monumental sum in those days. Unsure about the future of Waterloo, migrating Mennonite pioneers diverted their course to York County, where they founded the Markham colony. Meanwhile in Lancaster 23 farmers formed the German Land Company, which managed to raise the 10,000 dollars.

From 1805 until the War of 1812 and throughout the 1820's, an uninterrupted stream of Mennonites on foot, on horse-back, and in Conestoga wagons drawn by four- and six-horse teams moved along a 400-mile trail from different parts of Pennsylvania to the secured German Company Tract on the Grand River. The Mennonite demand for land was so great that in 1807 the German Company bought another 45,200 acres, known as the German Block, in Woolwich Township. By 1841, Upper Canada counted 5,400 Mennonite settlers (among a total population of 440,000): 3,000 of them in the Niagara District, 1,300 in and near Waterloo, 860 around Markham, and 140 along the northern shores of Lake Erie east of the Niagara District. The success of the Mennonite settlements enticed Tunkers and other Pennsylvania Dutch to follow them to Canada.

As pioneers who cleared and cultivated virgin land, built the first roads, bridges, churches, schools, and mills of all kinds, the German-speaking Mennonites were a significant factor in the formation of a fresh and unstructured country. The secret of their reputation as successful farmers has been their genuine love of the soil, which has led to their proper management of it through such practices as crop rotation. They were also successful community builders, who shared their German-language schools, their burial grounds, their skills as well as their resources with non-Mennonite, especially German-speaking settlers. Because at that time they emphas- ized the maintenance of their German culture as integral part of their faith, the Mennonites at the Grand River and in the Niagara District attracted almost the entire immigration from Germany from the 1830's to the 1850's and were thus responsible for the development of the concentrated German community in the Kitchener-Waterloo area. Without the Mennonite colonies, the German immigration would have dispersed throughout Canada.

The Mennonites in America

The Mennonite pioneers transplanted to Ontario both Anabaptist traditions and a century of German-American experience. In the history of German settlement in America the Mennonites had played a role similar to that in Canada. Thirteen Mennonite families from the Palatinate launched North America's first permanent German settlement in Germantown (now a part of Philadelphia) in 1683. They were soon joined by more Mennonite and non-Mennonite Germans. By 1750 the Mennonite community had grown to 5,000. Most of the newcomers were of Swiss-German origin. The exemplary farms they carved out of the wilderness along the Conestoga and Pequea rivers attracted more and more German immigrants to Lancaster, Montgomery, and Bucks counties. Mennonite pioneers spread German settlement to the south, east, and north of Lancaster and were the first Germans to cross the Allegheny Mountains. The covered Conestoga wagon was a Mennonite creation reflecting the ingenuity of their response to the challenges of pioneering. Sturdy and skilfully designed, it was devised by them in the 1730's for hauling their families and heavy, precious loads over long and hazardous distances. In Germantown William Rittenhouse built America's first paper mill and in 1726 a Mennonite named Kurtz erected America's first iron smelter. Mennonites are credited with the introduction of intensive agriculture in America and admired for transforming the lands occupied by them into the garden of Pennsylvania. Although they numbered no more than 5 percent of the Pennsylvania Dutch population of 100,000 in 1776, they laid the foundations for the flowering of a Pennsylvania Dutch community and culture -- the term "Dutch" (misunderstood from the German "deutsch") was a designation for Germans. The Mennonite impact on the economic development of this community has been recognized as exceptional.

Origins of the Mennonites

The Pennsylvania Mennonites who settled in Ontario around 1800 are also known as Swiss-German Mennonites, in contrast to the Dutch-German (also called Russian) Mennonites who settled in Manitoba in the 1870's. The mixture of southwest German dialects spoken by the Swiss-German Mennonites reveals their origin from the German-speaking lands along each side of the upper Rhine, while the Dutch-German or Russian Mennonites speak the Low German of West Prussia, where persecuted Anabaptists from northwestern Germany and the Netherlands had sought refuge since the 16th century. When they moved on from West Prussia to Russia in the 1780's, the originally Dutch, Flemish, and Friesian Mennonites preserved their acquired Low German language and culture until their resettlement in Canada one century later.

What unites these Anabaptists of different geographic and ethnic origins, apart from their German language, is their acceptance of the teachings of the Friesian Menno Simons (1496-1561), especially his insistence on passiveness and civil obedience. These were intended to induce greater tolerance towards the Anabaptists and soften their revolutionary image, an image that had targeted them as objects of ruthless and bloody persecution by all kinds of rulers. Nevertheless, the faith of the peaceful Mennonites -- particularly their refusal to accept infant baptism and to take oaths, their conscientious objection, their simple lifestyle, and their radically democratic beliefs and structures -- continued to be feared as a revolutionary force by the established churches, which they declined to join, and by governments, with whom they wanted little interaction. As late as 1715, Swiss Mennonites were arrested by the Calvinist governments of Zurich and Bern and sent as galley slaves to Italy or deported to Pennsylvania. Many found refuge in Alsace, the Palatinate, and Pennsylvania.

Despite persecution, Mennonite ranks were, from the beginning, divided by doctrinal disputes encouraged by their conviction that every believer was a priest and by conflicting interpretations of the only authourity they accepted -- the Gospel. Some of the early disputes were perpetuated in the New World, while some originated in North America as the result of renewal movements in the 19th century. In 1694 Swiss-Mennonite leader Jacob Amman started a breakaway movement, the Amish, by extending the ban (excommunication) to all those embracing such new social customs and fashions as shaven faces and long hair for men and fancy clothes and buttons. Because the Amish substituted hooks and eyes for buttons, which they associated with vanity, they were long called "hookers" *(Haftler)* and they themselves labelled the non-Amish Mennonites "buttoners" *(Knöpfler)*.

In 1712, Louis XV ordered the Amish expelled from their Alsatian homeland and forced them to scatter in Europe and North America. Today the divisions between the Amish and other Mennonites are still visible in their clothing and lifestyle. In the 19th century, Old Colony, Old Order (Wisler), Church of God in Christ Mennonites, and other branches have adopted Amish ways in varying degrees. Noticeable plain dress and horse-and-buggy-style of life are expressions of Mennonite refusal to conform to this world; they are a defence against the temptations of worldly pride and have a symbolic value in "bounding the community," as sociologist John E. Hostetler put it. As the modern world steadily encroached toward the borders of their communities, he argued, they often became more defensive of the old customs and tended to "freeze" them.

CHAPTER XXV

THE UNITED EMPIRE LOYALISTS

1. Founders of British Canada
2. German Loyalist settlements in Ontario
3. Loyalism among German Americans
4. Palatine migrations to New York

Founders of British Canada

The Loyalists were refugees from the American Revolution, forced to flee their American homes between 1775 (outbreak of hostilities) and 1783 (Treaty of Paris) because they supported or sympathized with the British Crown. They were condemned by the victorious American rebels, smeared in the press, dismissed from their occupations, and often vandalized and deprived of their possessions. The term "late Loyalists" applies to those who migrated to Canada after 1783 for reasons indirectly related to the American Revolution. Mennonites belong in this category. In Canada, *bona fide* Loyalists were offered free land and settlement provisions plus financial compensation for losses sustained in defence of the United Empire. The arrival of some 45,000 Loyalists (mostly members of Loyalists' corps, petty officials, and businessmen) with their families, particularly in the sparsely populated former British colonies of Nova Scotia and Québec, marks the beginning of the Canada we know. The territories of today's provinces received respectively: New Brunswick 14,000, Nova Scotia 5,000, Prince Edward Island 600, Cape Breton 400, Québec 6,800, and Ontario 20,000.

The coming of the Loyalists also marks the beginning of a national myth that has gradually petrified into a popular national dogma, particularly following the World War I experience. According to this myth, the Loyalists founded Canada on the virtues of conservative British sentiment and represent the alleged personification of Canada's British heritage. The myth that these political and war refugees were only pure English still persists. School texts, such as *Living in North America* (1986), define the Loyalists as "the first large group of English-speaking Canadians" and therefore the English, together with the French, as Canada's two "founding peoples". In British Canada the myth of the Loyalists' British origin has been espoused as one of the central symbols of Canadian nationalism, especially by the country's establishment. This has manifested itself in many ways, including the aspiration of many Canadians to be socially accepted in England, and the pride in being a British subject instead of a Canadian citizen.

It is indeed true that many Loyalists came from a British background. Equally indisputable, but generally unacknowledged, is historical evidence indicating that as many as half of Canada's Loyalist settlers were not of British descent and a large minority did not even speak English as their mother tongue. Most of the Loyalist refugees of British roots, including the principal political leaders, merchants, and landowners opposed to the Revolution, resettled in England, the West Indies and the Bahamas by 1783, leaving a cross-section of predominantly middle class American colonists (largely farmers, artisans, and a few former office-holders) as settlers in what was then Nova Scotia and Quebec. The Loyalists who stayed in Canada were, as the biographer of the Loyalist captain John W. Meyers noted, neither wealthy landowners nor lonely exiles, but frontiersmen who had pioneered before. They consisted of a broad spectrum of religious, ethnic, and racial minority groups -- such as Quakers, Huguenots, Tunkers, Lutherans, Reformed, German, Irish, Dutch, French, Scandinavians, Indians, and blacks. Estimates, based on names listed on land grants and select samples of Loyalists whose origins could be traced, put the percentage of Germans among the Loyalists in Canada within a range of from 10 percent to 30 per cent by 1784.

Some ethnic German Loyalists have become known through their biographies. One was Abraham Cunard, a very active member of the German Lutheran Church in Halifax. The founder of the famous Cunard Line was his successful merchant and shipbuilder son, Sir Samuel Cunard. Captain John Walden Meyers (also known as Walter Myers or Hans Waltermyer) from Albany has a commemorative plaque in his honour in Belleville, Ontario. He was feared among revolutionaries for his courageous raids. Swiss-born Peter Etter, a businessman from Boston, and Jacob Dittrick, grandson of a Palatine pioneer farmer from the Mohawk Valley, founded large family trees in Ontario. John Dulmage (Dolmetsch) and Paul Heck with their wives (both couples were Irish-born but German-speaking Palatinates) brought Methodism from Ireland to Camden Valley (near Albany) and, from there, introduced it to Canada in 1784.

German Loyalist settlements in Ontario

German Loyalists were found in the Maritimes, in Quebec, and in Ontario. In Quebec's Eastern Townships, near Mississquoi Bay, they founded Philipsburg, Freleghsburg, Noyan, and Potton. Most of them, however, appear to have settled in Ontario. The first German refugees from New York State are reported to have arrived in a starving condition at Fort George on the east bank of the Niagara, as early as 1776. Their party included 5 women and 34 children. At Fort Niagara, across the river in Canada, Butler's Rangers established their headquarters in 1777. Their first recruits were Palatine farmers from New York State. In order to provide supplies for the 300 men of his garrison and their refugee families who followed them, Colonel Butler started Upper Canada's first agricultural settlement in 1780. The family names of nearly 25 percent of the Loyalist resident families registered in Niagara in 1783 were German. They were among the first farmers in what seven years later became Upper Canada (Ontario). When Butler's Rangers were disbanded in 1784, the settlement, renamed Queenston, numbered 620 persons and grew rapidly. Historian William Kirby recorded that "half of those who came to the Niagara used the High or Low German and Dutch." The German Loyalist pioneers in Niagara drew Pennsylvania Dutch, Mennonites, Tunkers, and other German late Loyalist settlers to southwestern Ontario.

At the northeastern end of Lake Ontario an even larger number of disbanded German Loyalist troops became eastern Ontario's first European settlers in 1783. The majority were Lutherans. They can be credited with bringing the Lutheran church to Ontario. The early history of their congregations is the story of their determination to preserve their faith and their German language as long as possible. The idea of viable pioneer settlement in the virgin forest along the Bay of Quinte was apparently first suggested by Captain Michael Grass, a native of Germany from New York City who was familiar with the area. He was put in charge of relocating 900 Loyalists from New York to Kingston. Five Loyalist commanders (including Grass whose company contained the smallest number of Germans) of mostly German-American and Dutch volunteer troops, were allocated separate townships for each of their regiments east of Kingston. Their settlements were named Ernestown, Fredericksburgh, Adolphustown, and Marysburgh. In all four townships at least half of the original settlers were Palatine Loyalists. Marysburgh received a contingent of Hessians in 1785. Ernestown, with 2,300 inhabitants by 1811, became the most populous township in Ontario for awhile.

The heaviest concentration of German Loyalists, however, was found in four townships east of Kingston, namely Williamsburg, Matilda, Osnabruck, and Cornwall. Williamsburg and Matilda were wholly German. Their founders consisted of recruits from Sir John Johnson's first battalion of King's Royal Regiment of New York, a battalion composed almost entirely of Palatine farmers from the Mohawk and Schoharie. Johnson's regiment of 800 Germans and a few Scots had been stationed at Lake Champlain where their families joined them in 1783. According to one chronicler, more than 1,000 German Loyalists with their families moved to Upper Canada. Some historians have maintained that by giving Upper Canada's newly organized four districts the German names of Nassau, Hesse, Lunenburg, and Mecklenburg, Governor Lord Dorchester demonstrated a dual intention: he honoured the royal family's German connections and also recognized the large German element in the United Empire Loyalist population.

Loyalism among German Americans

American historians still disagree over the sympathies of the quarter of a million Germans living in the thirteen colonies at the time of the American Revolution. It must be kept in mind that German Americans do not want to be associated with the treasonous sympathies of Loyalists, just as many German Canadians proudly prefer to trace their ethnic roots to Loyalists. To counter the traditional view that Loyalism was negligible among German Americans in 1776, the argument has more recently been put forward that 25-40 percent of all Americans were opposed to the rebellion, including particularly Germans and Dutch who had retained their non-English culture. The evidence suggests that the German-American community was deeply divided. In the border areas of New York State, for instance, from where most of the identifiable German Loyalists originated, Germans under Nicolas Herchheimer are also celebrated as the leading proponents of the Revolution. Among the Palatine immigrants in New York's frontier region of the Hudson, Mohawk and Schoharie valleys, this dispute divided Germans of the same generation, from the same homelands, in the same settlements, and frequently from the same families. Most of the German Loyalists in the King's Royal Regiment were neighbours or tenants of Sir John Johnson's vast estates in the Mohawk River valley. Johnson himself, whose father had won over the Mohawk Indians to England's side, was of mixed Irish-German descent. His German neighbours sided with him in the revolution because of their allegiance to the Johnson family and their fear of a resumption of Indian raids.

Palatine migrations to New York

The bulk of German Loyalists who settled in Upper Canada were the children of a large party of Palatine emigrants of 1709-10 who had been subjected to a seemingly never-ending series of trials and tribulations in New York State. In the English-French wars the 2,000-3,000 Palatine farmers living at the edge of the wilderness on the Mohawk River frequently suffered loss of life to severe Indian raids. The governor of New York had encouraged the Palatines to settle in the

Mohawk wilderness in order to extend the state boundaries 40 miles westward. He intended for the settlers to be a barrier against hostile Indians. The farms they carved out of the Mohawk virgin forests in the 1720's had been the Palatines' third home in New York and their second effort to make a living as independent farmers. Most had been forced to abandon their first pioneer farms on the Schoharie when the governor of New York deliberately sold the land from under their feet to land speculators. Earlier, Indian chiefs had offered this land on the Schoharie to the impoverished immigrants who had been forced to burn pitch and tar for three years in Livingstone's Manor on the Hudson River after their arrival as indentured servants.

The Palatines had left Germany with the hope of becoming independent farmers in America. However, indentured servitude (i.e., having to work for others upon arrival for a specified time) was the price the 2,500 survivors from a party of 3,000 Palatines had agreed to pay for transatlantic passage from London to America. In London, where 14,000 southwest German emigrants waited in camps in 1709 to be transported to America, four visiting Mohawk Indian chiefs offered them land on the Schoharie for settlement. The English government permitted only 3,000 to go to New York and 850 to North Carolina; 2,900 were assigned places in Ireland and the rest, including all Roman Catholics, were returned to Germany. The descendants of some of those sent to Ireland migrated to the Mohawk valley in the 1760's and ended up as Loyalist settlers on Missisquoi Bay in 1784.

The flight in 1709 of 14,000 so-called Palatines from their southwest German homelands to London in search of a better life in America was an exodus unprecedented in scale. Experiencing crop failures, the ravages of the wars of Louis XIV, forcible religious conversions, exploitation by landlords, and oppression by their own rulers, common people from each side of the upper Rhine decided in 1709 to follow the optimistic advertisements of English and American recruiting agents exaggerating the advantages of the New World. Throughout 1709, a never-ending stream of near-starving Swiss, Alsatians, Badeners, Württembergers, Hessians, and Palatines moved through the Palatinate and Rotterdam to

London where they were accommodated in tents and fed at government expense for one year. Pitied at first and then disliked, "Palatines" became a pejorative English label for southwest German emigrants.

CHAPTER XXVI

THE HESSIANS

1. Historical significance of the "Hessians"
2. Hessian settlements in Canada
3. German troops in the American
   Revolutionary War
4. Recruiting German mercenaries for Canada

Historical significance of the "Hessians"

The label "Hessians" has been attached, somewhat inaccurately, to all of the estimated 30,000 German soldiers in British regiments in North America from 1776 to 1783. The British government had contracted on a business basis for these troops with the German princes of Hesse-Cassel, Brunswick, Hesse-Hanau, Ansbach-Bayreuth, Waldeck, and Anhalt-Zerbst to defend British interests against the threats of the American Revolution. Although these soldiers came from different parts of Germany, they all came to be called "Hessians" because the Hessian states supplied more than half of the troops. In American historical literature and popular mythology, "Hessians" is a derogatory term equated with German mercenaries who neither knew about nor cared for the issues of the American Revolution. "The average Yankee despised these peasants who had so docilely permitted their rulers to sell them at so much a head to fight another country's wars. They were the very personification of tyranny," states American historian Esther Forbes. The curse of the name "Hessian," as historians of America's Germans like Löher have stressed, "continues to be a stigma for all Germans in America, a label which the raw American throws with contempt into the face of honest Germans," regardless of

the sacrifices German Americans made for American independence.

Despite their negative American image the Hessians have
not received the publicity or credit due them in Canada. This
may be attributed to the fact that the Hessians were German
rather than British, and that they were connected with lost
battles for a lost cause.

In the context of Canadian history, however, they are
significant for two reasons. First, their arrival at a time when
the British force of 8,500 was dangerously outnumbered by
American rebel forces probably saved Canada for the British
Crown. The presence of the Hessians prevented the spreading
of the American Revolution to Quebec and Nova Scotia and
thus laid the foundation for the development of a Canadian
nation independent of the United States. Second, the Hessians
-- and particularly the estimated 2,400 Hessians who remained
in Canada after the war -- included highly skilled professionals, intellectuals, artists, and craftsmen who made notable
contributions to Canadian society. For instance, Canada
credits them with introducing the ancient German tradition
(dating back to at least 1509) of the Christmas tree. The
family of Baron von Riedesel, German commander of the
British forces, reportedly erected and lighted Canada's first
Christmas tree in 1781 at their residence in Sorel, Quebec.
Canada Post officially acknowledged this contribution 200
years later with a commemorative stamp in 1981.

Hessian settlements in Canada

Of the 30,000 German troops in North America known as
Hessians, slightly more than 10,000 were stationed on
Canadian soil during the war. An estimated 6,000 (some with
families) remained in North America after the war. Canada
became the new home for up to 2,400 of them, including some
who had served on American territory. At the same time,
many who had been stationed in Canada preferred settling in
the new United States. An estimated 1,400 Hessians settled in
Quebec and about 1,000 in Nova Scotia, New Brunswick, and
Ontario. Those who settled in Nova Scotia received free
transportation, 300 acres of land, and perks similar to the

Loyalists, whereas in Quebec and Upper Canada the Loyalists received better treatment with regard to land grants and the supply of provisions.

Since Halifax was a major base for Hessians throughout the war, it is not surprising to find Hessian settlements, such as Waldeck Line and Hessian Line (now Clementsvale), in Clements Township, Annapolis County. However, for the huge Lutheran church which they built in Clementsport in 1788 (known as the Loyalists' Church of St. Edward's) they never found a Lutheran pastor. Unsuited and unsuccessful as pioneer farmers on their original land grants, some of the Hessian and Ansbach veterans became servants to established German farmers in the Annapolis valley. Hessians also moved to places like Halifax and Lunenburg, where they mixed with the existing German population, as well as to Chester, Nine Mile River, and Digby. The group of 129 Hessians identified in Argyle and Shelburne in 1784 were reported to include 22 wives and 30 children. In New Brunswick, Hessians settled in Saint John and along the lower St. John River. They have even been traced among the early settlers of Prince Edward Island. In Quebec, Hessians were found in urban centres such as Montreal, Quebec, Trois Rivières, Sorel, and Chambly where they billeted during the war, as well as in small communities where they had wintered or received lands. In 1785, a contingent of about forty Hessians under Baron von Reitzenstein moved from Quebec to Lake Ontario to take up promised land in Marysburgh at the Bay of Quinte. Here they suffered great privations. They lacked experience in clearing the virgin forest and essential provisions, as well as social acceptance by their German Loyalist neighbours. Only their inability to finance another relocation compelled them to remain and make a living on their land and to form a Lutheran congregation together with the German Loyalists of the area.

The Hessian settlers are stated to have actually accounted for 3 to 4 percent of the entire male population of Canada in 1783. Their impact on the primitive Canadian society of the day was both cultural and demographic. French-Canadian historian Jean-Pierre Wilhelmy, himself a descendant of a Hessian soldier, points out that "in 1783 the French

Canadians were a largely uneducated lot; most of the
intellectuals and merchants had departed after the French
defeat of 1760. About 80 per cent of the population was rural.
One can well imagine, then, how the influx of qualified
soldiers, with their wealth of experience gleaned through
service in a highly disciplined army, affected the social and
economic picture of the time. Army doctors, merchants of
every kind, men from every craft and profession, musicians
and heaven knows what else, all of them broadened by their
military experience, occupied a variety of important posts and
contributed to the development of our country through the
practice of their skills." Since most of the Hessians arrived
single and married the daughters of local residents, they
assimilated rapidly. True to the proverbial French-Canadian
fertility, Hessians who married French-Canadian wives sometimes had families with as many as 14 to 18 children. Within a
few generations, the Hessians thus bequeathed to Canada tens
of thousands of descendants.

German troops in the American Revolutionary War

England's decision to hire initially 20,000 European
mercenaries wherever they could be obtained -- from Russia,
Holland, or Germany -- to fight the American rebellion was
taken when rebel forces were invading Canada in order to
capture Quebec. With an army of little more than 8,000 men
in North America and an additional 37,000 men scattered
around the rest of the British Empire, the British government
had been caught woefully unprepared in 1775. It feared not
only the loss of its North American possessions but also an
invasion of the militarily denuded British Isles by France and
Spain. Throughout the War of Independence the number of
German troops on Britain's side equalled that of the English
troops and, for two years, as Canada's Governor Haldimand
wrote to Lord Germain, his "English" army was for the most
part German. "For a period of seven critical years," to quote
historian Charles S. Blue, "Canada was largely dependent on
German troops, not only for her defence, but for the active
prosecution of a campaign in which her interests and integrity
were seriously imperilled. They garrisoned her cities and forts,
transformed her villages into cantonments, took part in her

battles." Alongside the Hessians fought Loyalist militia which (as explained in chapter XXV) also included a high proportion of first- and second-generation German immigrants.

On the American side, there were also a number of regiments consisting exclusively of German Americans, and a large part of the American forces were led by German officers. Furthermore, the French auxiliary troops that came to the aid of the American Revolution included units consisting entirely of ethnic Germans from the French border areas of Zweibrücken, Trier, the Saar, Alsace, and Lorraine. Since two thirds of the Hessians were stationed and in action on American territory throughout the war, Germans inevitably were fighting Germans on many occasions. For instance, in the New Jersey campaign of 1778, Hessians under Baron von Knyphausen faced Baron von Steuben, both officers having served as comrades under Frederick the Great of Prussia. In the 1781 siege of Yorkton, Germans fought under three flags: soldiers of Hesse and Ansbach-Bayreuth under the British flag were pitted against Armand's Legion of Germans from Pennsylvania, under Steuben, as well as against the Royal German Regiment of Zweibrücken under the French flag. A victorious Palatine officer of the Zweibrücken regiment complimented the captured troops from Hesse-Cassel for having "served throughout this war with the greatest distinction." The historical evidence given in the scholarly accounts of Gradish, Eelking, Kipping, Kügler, Lowell, and Atwood confirms that the "Hessians" in the American war were excellent soldiers who fought with valour and great gallantry. Although several thousand elected to stay in America after the war, desertion during the war was apparently not as prevalent among them as among the British, Americans, and German Americans.

Recruiting German mercenaries for Canada

A stubbornly surviving lore has it that the corruption and greed of German rulers motivated the Hessians' involvement in Britain's cause, that beggars, cripples, criminals, and foreigners were indiscriminately pressed into service, and even innocent travellers and heads of families were kidnapped for this purpose. The scorn for this alleged unique sale of the lives and services of German subjects to the highest bidder has also affected the historical judgment of the quality and performance of the Hessian troops. What may be held responsible for this rather negative image of the Hessians was the awakening in Germany of liberal and national consciousness, which, in turn, resulted from the American and French Revolutions. Reflecting 19th-century liberal and nationalist sentiment, historians such as Kapp, Löher, and Cronau were embarrassed by the role that Germany had played in the American struggle for freedom.

In reality, the hiring of the Hessians and the recruiting of uprooted people was in no way exceptional for the times because the commerce in troops had been a centuries-old European tradition. In 1760 the 90,000 men in the British army included 68,000 Germans (37,800 Hannoveranians, 24,400 Hessians, and 9,500 Brunswickers). Most of the Hessian troops sent to America in 1776 were regulars, and recruitment was, on the whole, selective and non-compulsory. Only after 1779, when it was difficult to replace those who had been captured or killed, was recruitment extended to unemployed and vagrants, or were some individuals impressed against their will, such as the writer Gottfried Seume. However, even such recruiting methods were not uncommon elsewhere in Europe then. It was a widely shared view in western Europe at the time that recruitment siphoned off from society all the vagabonds who would otherwise become thieves and murderers.

Although many recruits seized the opportunity to plan their emigration to America and, for this reason, insisted on taking their wives with them (an estimated 200-250 German women accompanied their soldier husbands to Canada), few were adequately informed about America. Canada was virtually unknown in Europe at the time, and the reports and letters from the officers and men provided Germany with its first detailed information about Canada.

CHAPTER XXVII

THE MORAVIANS

1. David Zeisberger and the mission among
   the Indians
2. Cultural work among the Labrador Inuit
3. Origin and significance of the Labrador
   mission

David Zeisberger and the mission among the Indians

The Moravians, also known as *Unitas Fratrum* (literally: The
Unity of Brethren), are a Protestant group who believe that
the ethical principles of the Scriptures, such as love, rather
than dogmatic formulation of creed, must govern Christian
conduct as evidence of salvation. They trace their denominational roots to John Hus, the Czech reformer burned at the
stake in 1415. In the 16th and 17th centuries his followers had
their faith suppressed. They were severely persecuted and
nearly decimated until they experienced a renewal in 1772
under the patronage of a pietist Lutheran nobleman in
Saxony, Count Nicholas Louis von Zinzendorf. Offering
Moravians a haven on his estate where he built the
community called Herrnhut for them (hence their German
name *Herrnhuter*), Zinzendorf converted to their faith and
became their spiritual leader. He gave them the vision to
become not just another Protestant church but a union of
spiritually like-minded brethren within existing Protestant
churches. They should be, he advocated, primarily dedicated
to taking the Gospel to the far corners of the globe, especially
to the oppressed and neglected native peoples. The missionaries "had to be willing to serve without pay, to work for
their living, to be content with bare necessities, and to suffer,

die and be forgotten, content that such was the will of God."
In 1732 the first Moravian missionaries went to the black
slaves of the West Indies and in 1733 to the Inuit (Eskimos)
of Greenland.

In 1735 Moravians visited America, inspired by the ideals of
converting the Indians and bringing about a spiritual union of
America's Protestant churches. Although the latter objective
was bound to fail, the Moravian church -- of all the German
churches in America -- was the first and for some time the
only one that cared for the fate of black slaves and the native
Indian and Inuit peoples of North America. The missionaries
travelled extensively through frontier settlements, built mission posts in the wilderness, and became the most successful
missionaries of American Indians. In addition, they had a
tradition of being pioneers in education. One of their last
pre-Herrnhut bishops, John Amos Comenius, who died in
1670, is widely considered the "father of modern education."
He was invited to be the first president of Harvard but
declined. In keeping with their encouragement of literacy for
both sexes, the Moravians opened boarding schools for
females as well as males in their first American communities
of Bethlehem and Nazareth (1741), Lititz (1747) and others;
the schools have been recognized as among America's first
and best in those days.

Canada was associated with the most outstanding Moravian
missionary among the Indians, David Zeisberger (1721-1808).
His sixty-three years of service among the Indians constitutes
the longest missionary career on record and earned him the
title "Apostle to the Indians." Speaking Delaware, Mohawk,
and five other Indian languages, he gave the Indians
instruction in English and German, compiled the first
Delaware, Iroquois, and Algonquin dictionaries, and taught
the Delaware to read and write their own language. From the
1740's he ministered to the Indians in the Canadian-American
border areas of Ohio and settled converted Christian Indians
in six communities. Although he taught and practiced
pacifism, he and his converted Indians were frequently
unjustly penalized by both sides for suspected collaboration
with the enemy. In the notorious massacre of 1782 American
militiamen cruelly killed the entire non-resisting Moravian
Indian population of Salem and Gnadenhuetten.

In 1791, 150 surviving Indians from the former New Salem congregation of 400 fled with Zeisberger to Canada, where they were offered land and assistance to form the prosperous colony of Schoenfeldt (known in English as Fairfield) near present-day Thamesville in Kent County, Ontario. In 1798 Zeisberger, a man totally dedicated to his Indian ministry, reluctantly acquiesced to pressures of the American government and the Moravian bishop of Bethlehem to return to the United States to begin the colony of Goshen, Ohio. He left behind most of his Indian converts who, considering him their spiritual leader, continued the mission until 1903. Their descendants still live on the Moravian Indian Reserve he founded near Thamesville.

Cultural work among the Labrador Inuit

On the coast of northern Labrador (since 1763 a part of Newfoundland), the Moravians can look back on a more than two-hundred-year record of spiritual, cultural, and material endeavours for the benefit of the Inuit. In the absence of any other civilizing force (such as government agencies, police, medical, or social services) until the mid-20th century, the history of the northern half of Labrador has been, as the Rev. F.W. Peacock experienced it as late as the eve of World War II, "the history of the Moravian missions on the Coast." Until 1946, when the Newfoundland government assumed supervision of the Moravian schools, the Moravians were entirely responsible for the education of the Labrador Inuit. Along a rugged, barren, and inhospitable coastline of some 1,000 miles Moravians established -- between 1752 and 1900 -- eight mission stations, which represented the only outposts of western civilization in that part of the world.

In 1900, at the peak of its operations, the Labrador mission counted a total missionary staff of 37 (including missionaries' wives) and a following of a fairly constant number of about 1,000 baptized Inuit (from an estimated population of 1,500 Inuit along the entire Labrador coast) and 200-300 so-called settlers (i.e., whites or half-Inuit). The latter were found around the southernmost station of Makkovik, which was built in 1896 primarily to serve "settlers," whose numbers were increasing as the Inuit along the coast were decreasing. By 1900, the seasonal Labrador fishery of Newfoundland fishermen, which began around 1860 and by 1900 involved 30,000 to 40,000 fishermen, became a growing concern and focus of Moravian attention. These fishermen, Moravian deacon Schulze observed, "behaved as crude and ignorant people to whom religion was almost totally unknown. They became a real danger for the Eskimos." From the outset, the missionaries had viewed with apprehension the exposure of the Inuit to the unscrupulous exploitation by independent traders. Penetrating Labrador from the south, the traders' and fishermen's spiritually and socially corrosive influence on Inuit culture presented itself as the frightening alternative to the effort of the Moravians.

The Inuit were a nomadic people who hunted and fished for their livelihood in the far North during the summer months. Since the Moravians did not want to disrupt the nomadic lifestyle, they confined contacts with the Inuit to the winter when these camped around the mission stations. Contacts, nevertheless, were pervasive because the Moravians had to assume a twofold role as religious teachers and the purveyors of the Inuits' external comfort. Furthermore, the missionaries had to act as employers, traders, judges, and mediators. Natives were reimbursed for services rendered and trade was organized as an educational means for teaching natives how to manage their resources. For more than a century the missionaries provided the only qualified medical care against the infections and diseases spread from contacts with Europeans and Newfoundlanders in southern Labrador.

Literacy was a high priority for the Moravians. Accordingly, they established the first school in Labrador in 1791, and by 1843, most of the Inuit were literate in their own language. Based on their work for the Greenland Inuit, the missionaries created a written language (Inuktut), grammar, an Inuit dictionary, and a translation of the Scriptures for the Labrador Inuit. Lacking Inuit equivalents for many of the spiritual concepts and everyday items necessary to teach the Gospel, the German missionaries who undertook this pioneer work had to create a large body of new Inuit vocabulary. As a byproduct, German words like *Gott, heilig, Löwe, Taube,*

Harfe, Kartoffel, counting *eins, zwei, drei...* and the German names for the days of the week entered the native language.

Since 1815, the Moravian school curriculum in Labrador included history, geography, political, and social studies. In 1822, Inuit were introduced to European musical instruments and showed such skill and enthusiasm that, according to the Reverend Peacock, it was not uncommon until recently to meet an Inuk who could play two or three brass instruments, the organ, and three stringed instruments. Among the missionaries were amateur scientists and skilled artisans who taught the Inuit a variety of arts and crafts, including optics, electromagnetism, and the use of nets for catching seals.

The Moravians imparted to the Inuit many German customs and traditions. Among these are the celebration of Christmas with the decorated tree, the exchange of gifts on Christmas Eve, and the German love for music in the form of choirs, brassbands, string quartets, and classical music concerts. Until World War II, the organization of social and cultural life at the mission stations was as German as the physical layout and architectural style of the mission buildings because until then most of the Moravian missionaries in Labrador were of German background and had trained in Germany.

Due to their training, wide range of interests and educational approach, the Moravians have contributed much to our knowledge of the Inuit and their environment. They systematically observed and collected almost everything and communicated the findings for evaluation and publication to scholars in Germany. For example, they collected information about the geography, climate, flora, fauna, and other natural phenomena, thereby enabling scholars in Germany to conduct further scientific studies. With the missionaries' help, the renowned entomologist Heinrich Benno Möschler was able to publish from 1848 to 1870 what was the first and today still is one of the most comprehensive classifications of Labrador butterflies. The meteorological field work that Prof. K.R. Koch carried out on a visit to the Nain mission station in 1882 constituted Germany's contribution to the international polar year of 1882-83. The missionaries' geological curiosity led them to discover the semi-precious blue stone called Labradorite, and their cartographic skills yielded the first

accurate maps (the Reichel map was in use until 1957) of the
coastline of northern Labrador. The British search party for
Sir John Franklin's expedition of 1850-52 included the
German Okak missionary Miertsching, whose linguistic
expertise made him invaluable.

Origin and significance of the Labrador mission

The Moravian venture in Labrador would have been
impossible without the encouragement of the British government and the assistance of the Society for the Furtherance of
the Gospel (S.F.G.), a Moravian association in London.
Labrador, formerly a part of New France, had become
annexed to British Newfoundland following the Peace of Paris
in 1763, and the British were anxious to pacify the native Inuit
so that English fishermen could exploit the rich fishing
grounds off the Labrador coast without interference. The
S.F.C., which also had a commercial interest in the trade with
the Labrador natives, took responsibility for financing the
mission and its material needs. A group of merchants within
the S.F.G. bought a supply vessel and fitted it out for an
annual voyage to the mission stations.

The idea of extending the Moravian ministry to the Labrador
Inuit, who were reputed to be (in the words of Newfoundland
Governor Palliser) "the most treacherous, cruel and barbarous of all savages ever known," was initiated by Moravian
missionaries in Greenland. They were convinced that the same
transformation of the lives of the Inuit could be wrought in
Labrador as in Greenland, and they attributed the Inuits' bad
reputation to conflicts arising from their trade with European
(before 1763, mostly French) fishing, trading, and naval
partners in the south. The great difficulties of establishing a
mission in Labrador became clear in 1752 when local Inuit
murdered seven members of a Moravian exploratory party led
by the Mecklenburg sailor John Christian Erhardt (labelled
"the Dutchman" by Anglo-Saxon chronists). Earlier in that
year he had helped select a mission site near present-day
Hopedale. Although a house built on this site in 1752 became
the first mission station, it was subsequently abandoned.

The first permanent mission station was finally built in 1771; the site chosen was Nain. This happened only after further voyages of exploration in the 1760's and the British government's approval of a land grant of 100,000 acres (to prevent fishermen and traders from interfering with the Moravians) in 1769. The excellent progress the missionaries were able to make in their relations with the Inuit caused the British government to approve a second mission station called Okak to the north in 1775 and a third one named Hoffenthal (Hopedale) to the south in 1782 near the first abandoned station. Five more stations along the coast were opened during the 19th century. Since the natives tended to resume their old beliefs when migrating, the missionaries realized that they must go where the natives went and gathered.

In the long run, of course, the mission could not and did not intend to provide a complete substitute for the southern trader and for the inevitably increasing contacts with modern society. Today's Anglo-Canadian social scientists tend to be critical of the Moravians' endeavours. The Moravians are blamed for allegedly ruining indigenous Inuit culture and encouraging the Inuit to adopt an alien settled pattern of life. Some critics go as far as holding the Moravian Church responsible for epidemics and disasterous population decline among the Inuit, arguing that the missionaries destroyed the traditional health care system and viewed suffering and death as desirable. Such arguments, however, cannot invalidate the overriding benefits Moravians brought to the Inuit. Summarizing the well-documented findings of historical research, historian William H. Whiteley concludes that "it is due in no small measure to the efforts of the Brethren that the Eskimos in Labrador have survived and prospered, rather than being hunted down and exterminated as were the native Beothucks of Newfoundland."

CHAPTER XXVIII

THE LUNENBURG GERMANS

1. The first German-Canadian community
2. Pioneers in Nova Scotia
3. The Halifax community
4. Recruiting the "foreign Protestants"

The first German-Canadian community

No open-minded, inquisitive visitor to Lunenburg County, Nova Scotia, can fail to notice the seemingly indelible stamp left upon the region by the distinctive folk culture of 18th-century Germans. Although the German language itself disappeared nearly a century ago, the so-called "Lunenburg Dutch" dialect, i.e., a peculiar accent and unusual phrasing, is still detectable in Lunenburg County English, as are elements of German folklore and folk beliefs. In the Lunenburg countryside, a number of German customs have not died out. One is the Christmas custom of "belsnickling" and another the old southwest German tradition of working with and exhibiting teams of oxen, decked out with brass-tipped horns and harnesses decorated with heart-shaped brass medallions. Apart from artifacts and decorative designs in furniture and on utensils and fabrics, the aspects of German heritage most alive today in the Lunenburg area are the Lutheran faith and the cherished foods -- homemade sausages, sauerkraut, potato soup, and pudding -- brought by the original settlers from Germany.

All these relics of German culture point to a once flourishing German community life. They also attest to the vitality and adaptability of this first permanent German-speaking settlement on Canadian soil. In other parts of present-day Canada lived in or visited by individuals or small groups of German origin since the 16th century, comparable traces have vanished. The significance of the Lunenburg and Halifax Germans from the perspective of German-Canadian history lies in their development of the first German community life in Canada. Not only did they organize their own church and school and adhere to their inherited customs and lifestyle for more than century, but they also adapted successfully to the new economic and geographic challenges of the area.

Although they arrived as farmers and labourers from the landlocked southwest of German-speaking Europe, they began to add fishing and boatbuilding to their farming skills immediately after they settled along the coast of Nova Scotia. Within thirty years they built vessels up to 35 tons in size to sail as far as the coast of Labrador. The Zwicker Company was in the fishing business from 1789 to 1959. Its import-export business produced saltfish, exported it to the West Indies, and imported rum, coffee, molasses, and tobacco. The Smith and Rhuland Shipyard (built in 1850) turned out some of the best and fastest schooners and yachts. It became known for launching the famous Bluenose I in 1921, which won every sailing competition in the North Atlantic. Lunenburgers were in the forefront of developing new technologies in boatbuilding and fishing in the Maritimes. In 1869, Lunenburg fishermen successfully introduced trawling or longlining which made offshore fishing profitable. Four years later the 58-ton Lunenburg vessel *Dielytris* (manned by skippers Loye, Hirtle, and Geldert) became the first boat to spend a complete season fishing on the "banks" in the deep sea between Nova Scotia and Newfoundland, as well as off Labrador. This marked the beginning of the banks fishery, which saw up to 150 vessels from Lunenburg sail to the banks annually by 1900. Their return every September has become the occasion for Lunenburg's most celebrated event of the year, the Fisheries' Exhibition, or Fishermen's Picnic.

Pioneers in Nova Scotia

Since the Lutheran Church was the centre of the Germans'

community life, the cultural and economic transformation of the community can be traced in the language of the church services, the declining membership of the Lutheran in relation to the Anglican congregation, and in the increasing listing of fisherman instead of farmer as the occupation of the father in the baptismal registers. It can thus be shown that the transition of the Lunenburg Germans from a people primarily working the land to a people oriented chiefly towards the sea coincided with the disappearance of the German mother tongue in favour of English after the middle of the 19th century. The adoption of fishing and shipbuilding rendered obsolete and inappropriate much of both their transplanted agricultural language as well as their inherited farming customs and folklore. In addition, the inland German language they had brought with them was lacking marine vocabulary. The German language faded even more when, unlike the Kitchener-Waterloo area, the original German settlers of Halifax and Lunenburg received no regenerating infusion of German-speaking immigrants after the American Revolutionary War.

The significant question, therefore, is not why German began to disappear after the third or fourth generation, but why, in contrast to the Hessian and Loyalist settlements in Canada, it survived for more than a century to leave traces until even today. To appeciate the cultural vitality of the Lunenburg Germans, we must realize that their cohesion was forged and tested in the challenges of pioneering land settlement, the founding of a new community, and the building of a new church.

The obstacles faced by the heterogeneous group of 2,400 so-called "foreign Protestants" who had arrived from Germany by 1753 were indeed formidable. To begin with, they came from different social groups and from hundreds of towns and villages belonging to all the states situated between Geneva and the North Sea coast, but particularly from the regions on each side of the upper Rhine, and included some French and Dutch. In 1753 this motley group was anything but a community. Second, arriving as destitute indentured servants or "redemptioners," they had to work off their passage debts as government labourers in Halifax before they could organize their lives into a community as independent farmers. Third, the 1,400 of them assigned farms around the site of Lunenburg in 1753 first had to fortify it. Their settlements in the Lunenburg area were threatened by the ongoing war with the French until 1758, ravaged by hostile Indians until 1760, and raided by Americans during the American Revolutionary War.

Their Lutheran faith was the overriding factor for more than a century in the active retention of their heritage. Despite pressures from the Church of England to claim the new immigrants, the Lunenburg Germans stubbornly clung to their Lutheran religion and, after intricate maneuvering, succeeded in obtaining their own Lutheran church, pastor, and German-language service by 1770. Zion Evangelical Lutheran Church of Lunenburg is the oldest surviving Lutheran church in Canada today. The Lunenburg Lutheran minister organized social and cultural activities, including a German school in the 1760's, and again after 1782. In the 1780's and 1790's German settlers who had moved to the surrounding areas came to the services in Lunenburg, but in the 19th century the Lunenburg Lutheran pastors also preached in the growing German communities nearby. English-speaking assistant Lutheran ministers did not appear until 1877. The Lutheran Church was thus a focal point encouraging social cohesion among the German immigrants and the preservation of the German cultural heritage in Lunenburg County.

The Halifax community

After the departure of the 1,400 settlers from Halifax to Lunenburg in 1753, Halifax still had a German population of 1,000. From the early 1750's Lutheran services were held in a little schoolhouse still standing today on the corner of Gerrish and Brunswick Streets. This schoolhouse, transformed into "the little Dutch church" and dedicated as St. George's in 1761, was the first Lutheran church on Canadian soil. After declining to 264 in 1766, the German population in Halifax (whose total population estimates vary from 1,300-3,000 in 1763-66) expanded again to well over 1,000 with the influx of Loyalist refugees and disbanded Hessians in the 1770's and

1780's. From 1788 to 1801 Anton Heinrich published the
Neu-Schottländischer Calender, Canada's first German-
language periodical and first ethnic newspaper, in Halifax. The
German influx also resulted in the opening of a German
school, operated jointly by Lutherans and Reformed, and the
launching of Canada's first German secular association, the
"High German Society," which functioned from 1786 to 1791.
Its secretary was the Hessian officer Adolph Christoph Veith.
Veith played a notable role in both the Halifax municipal
administration and St. George's Church, even after the
Lutheran and German character of its congregation became
Anglican and English around 1800. Although Halifax's
German-speaking population had been largely assimilated or
dispersed by the 1830's, the long-used designation of "Dutch
Town" for the original German residential sector, as well as
various German street names (for example Brunswick Street,
Bauer Street, and Dresden Row) are reminiscent of the
presence of a significant German community for three
quarters of a century after the founding of the city.

Although 18th- and early 19th-century historical records
(such as the 1760 Halifax resident quoted in Haliburton's
account of 1829), characterized local Germans as "the most
industrious and useful settlers amongst us," few histories of
Nova Scotia acknowledge the stabilizing role played by the
so-called "foreign Protestants" in the crucial, uncertain
formative period of Nova Scotian history. In the early 1750's,
these "foreigners" outnumbered the English in Nova Scotia
and, after the abrupt expulsion of the francophone Acadians
in 1755, the communities of Lunenburg and Halifax (with its
partially German population) were the only European
settlements left in Nova Scotia for several years.

Recruiting the "foreign Protestants"

The organized shipment of German "foreign Protestants"
during 1750-53 to populate Halifax and Lunenburg was one of
several government schemes Britain entertained to strengthen
its precarious position in Nova Scotia vis-a-vis the francophone, Roman Catholic Acadians. It was the third and most
significant appearance of Germans into the colony within a
five-year period.

The first instance resulted from the successful capture of Louisbourg from France in 1745. The Boston merchant Samuel Waldo was instrumental in organizing this with a large number of Germans whom he had settled earlier on his estate in Maine in a place called Waldoburg. Accompanied by their families, the German victors then founded a settlement near Louisbourg which they also called Waldoburg. It was the first German settlement on Canadian soil. However, these settlers had to be evacuated in 1748 when Louisbourg was returned to the French by the Treaty of Aix-la-Chapelle. Some of Waldo's Germans moved on to Halifax. One of them, Sebastian Zauberbühler, was named a magistrate by the governor and sent to Lunenburg where he was elected to the first House of Assembly in 1758. Germans of the Royal American regiment later participated in the final capture of Louisbourg in 1758. Many of them, such as Anton Heinrich, became prominent members of the Halifax German community.

The second group of Germans came as a result of the British decision to found Halifax in 1749. The British objective was to counter the controlling position of French Louisbourg. They brought discharged soldiers and London paupers to be the first residents. These proved unsuitable as settlers, except for a few Swiss and Germans among them, like Otto Wilhelm Schwartz and Philip August Knaut, who later assisted in the settling of the Lunenburg Germans. Governor Cornwallis was apparently so impressed with the high quality of the few "Swiss" among his "English rabble" that he asked the Lords of Trade in London to recruit more of the same kind of Protestants as settlers for Nova Scotia.

Foreign Protestants from continental Europe were readily available as immigrants and they became the largest group of German settlers coming to Canada in that period. Events like the revocation of the Edict of Nantes (1685), the mass flight of Palatines (1709), and the expulsion of Protestants from Salzburg (1731-32) were producing a continuous stream of mainly German-speaking refugees eager to emigrate to North America. By the 1740's German emigrants, variously lumped together by the English under such labels as "Palatines," "Dutch," or "Swiss," had already established a reputation as excellent settlers in British colonial Pennsylvania. The settling of Nova Scotia, therefore, appeared to the British authorities in 1749-50 simply a matter of deflecting an already strong current of German migrants flowing to Pennsylvania and Carolina. All that appeared necessary was the offering of attractive conditions, such as free passage and land.

The business of recruiting the settlers was transferred to an agent named Dick of Rotterdam. He received a commission for each emigrant he recruited. For this he employed a subagent named Köhler in Frankfurt on the Main. They, like the other recruiting agents with whom they competed for the flourishing emigrant trade, were interested solely in financial gain and not in the welfare of the emigrants. Not surprisingly, therefore, Dick and Köhler used highly unrealistic and deceptive descriptions of conditions in Nova Scotia to attract settlers. However, the prospective emigrants were so eager to become free landowners in America that those too destitute to pay for their passage in advance were willing to follow the mid-18th century practice of indenturing themselves, i.e., contracting to sell their labour for a specified time upon arrival in the New World. On the overcrowded emigrant ships sailing from Rotterdam to Halifax, such unsanitary conditions prevailed that during the long (from 70 to 120 days) and hazardous trips from 1750 to 1753 between 5 and 15 percent, i.e., an average of 9.4 percent, of the passengers died. Many more died after disembarkation from prolonged malnutrition, exhaustion, and diseases contracted on board.

After their trials and tribulations, the immigrants were understandably not eager to work for years in abject conditions as labourers on public construction projects in Halifax. Before they had completely paid off their passages with labour, they demanded and were given the free land promised them before their departure from Europe. Major Charles Lawrence, who supervised their relocation from Halifax to Lunenburg in 1753 noted: "Absurd and outrageous as these people in their dispositions are, I must yet do them the justice to observe that they are indefatigable when laboring for themselves... they must, I think, in spite of themselves, become a flourishing people and fulfill the public every expectation formed concerning them."

CHAPTER XXIX

EARLY QUEBEC

1. Germans in early 19th-century Quebec
2. In French and English service, 1711-1776
3. Settlers in 17th-century New France

Germans in early 19th-century Quebec

The founding of the *Deutsche Gesellschaft zu Montreal* in 1835, Quebec's first German society, revealed the presence of several different generations of Quebecers of German descent. They belonged to three or four different periods of immigration and (as the minutes of the founders' meeting indicate) held different positions in society and spoke different mother tongues (French, English, or German). Louis Gugy, the society's first president, and Daniel Arnoldi, the first vice-president, were French Canadians of Swiss-German and German descent who traced their roots in Quebec to the period before 1776. Secretary John C. Gundlach and charter members Schiller, Bohle, and Fensterwald were descendants of the "Hessians" who had fought for Britain during the Revolutionary War of 1775-1783. Musician J.C. Brauneis represented the generation that had arrived at the time of the War of 1812; society co-founders Meyer, Bower, Albeck, Seybold, Idler, Hetz, and Schmidt (the last six were natives of Württemberg) belonged to the most recent wave of immigrants from Germany.

While a high proportion of the most recent immigrants of the 1830's engaged in such practical occupations as butcher, innkeeper, and grocer, some among the oldest group descending from pre-1776 immigrants had assimilated into the anglophone ruling elite and occupied top positions as servants

of the Crown, administrators, and merchants. Many descendants of the Hessian soldiers, on the other hand, had
assimilated into French-Canadian society, where they ranked
prominently as professionals and artists. It is therefore not
surprising that the Rebellion of 1837 saw German Quebecers
divided in their loyalties. Sheriff Gugy, government physician
Arnoldi, officers Maximilian Globensky, and George de
Rottenburg, along with other residents of German origin,
helped to organize the opposition to the rebels, whose ranks
contained French-Canadian patriots descending from the
Hessians and other German-speaking immigrants, such as the
executed Swiss-born rebel Hindelang. The Swiss had been a
strong component of Quebec's German and French communities from the beginning. In addition, under the French-
Swiss-born Governor General of Canada, Sir George Prévost
(1767-1816), German Swiss had settled in substantial numbers
after the disbanding of the Swiss Regiments de Meuron and
de Watteville, which had fought for Canada in the War of
1812.

Few know that Baron Francis de Rottenburg (1757-1832),
father of the above mentioned Baron George de Rottenburg
and a native of Danzig, was the commander of the Quebec
garrison in 1810 and of all the British forces responsible for
the defence of Lower Canada in 1812 during the War of 1812.
He had entered French military service in 1782, joined the
unsuccessful rising of Polish patriots as an officer in 1794, and
afterwards organized the King's Royal Rifle Corps, the first
rifle battalion of German *Jäger* in the British army. His son
George, fluent in French and one of the chief organizers of
the Canadian militia, was its top ranking officer by 1855. He
became commander of the popular Prince of Wales' Royal
Canadian Regiment which he raised in Canada. George so
completely vanished from public recollection that his death in
1894 went unnoticed by the media.

German artists, scientists, and professionals figure prominently among Quebec's cultural elite in the early 19th
century. Musicians Friedrich Glackemeyer (bandmaster of
Baron von Riedesel's troops), Franz Vogler, Theodor F. Molt,
and Johann Christoph Brauneis brought professional stan-
dards of classical music to Quebec as teachers, organists,
composers, and importers of musical instruments. The

thirty-six or so Hessian surgeons who stayed in Canada after 1783 and the descendants of German medics from earlier wars (especially the Arnoldi brothers and Henry Loedel) laid the foundation in the 1820's for the organization of Quebec's medical profession and a medical school that became McGill University. In the art of portrait and landscape paintings, which Hessian descendant Henry Ritter and William von Moll Berczy had raised to high levels in Quebec, the work of German-born and -trained Cornelius Krieghoff gained national fame.

In French and English service, 1711-1776

The British conquest of French Canada in 1760 divides the period between the first British draft of German immigrants (three hundred Palatines from the upper Hudson River) for a campaign against Quebec in 1711 and the arrival of the Hessians in 1776. After 1760, the British opened up conquered Quebec to non-French immigrants and facilitated the rise of German settlers to social and economic prominence. Prior to 1760, the feudal order of Quebec deterred non-French settlement, but in pursuit of the intermittent struggle for the control of North America, both the English and the French sides had enlisted the services of Swiss and German soldiers and officers, some of whom stayed in Quebec.

As warriors, diplomats, and administrators, Swiss and Germans were reputed to be reliable and efficient. Popular nationalism was unknown in Germany prior to the French Revolution and Germans served loyally, whether under the English or the French Crown. Consequently, in North America as in Europe, at times Germans fought Germans. This happened, for instance, in 1745 when Samuel Waldo's Palatines laid siege to and conquered the French fortress of Louisbourg, which was garrisoned and defended by Swiss-German troops of the Karrer regiment. In the 1755 Battle of Lake George, Sir William Johnson of New York (of Irish descent but married to the German Katharina Weissenbach -- their offspring included the famous Loyalist Sir John Johnson) defeated French forces under their supreme commander, the Saxon Baron von Dieskau. Von Dieskau had come from

Europe in 1755 with 3,000 fresh troops. General Wolfe's decisive attack on Quebec in 1759 brought heavy losses to the Royal American Regiment, which contained large numbers of Palatine soldiers.

Swiss-born Sir Frederick Haldimand, who had served in the Prussian army during the War of the Austrian Succession (1740-45) and as an officer of the Royal Americans from their beginning in 1756, was the most illustrious of the British Crown's servants of German origin. He rose from second in command of the British forces in 1760, to become military governor of Montreal and Trois Rivières from 1760-64, and Governor-General of Quebec from 1776 to 1786. He attained his position because of his loyal, competent service to the Crown and the lack of similarly qualified British candidates. His biographers (S.R.J. Sutherland et al.) note that as late as 1775, the British authorities still considered him a "Swiss mercenary" and a "foreigner" and that he owed the honour of being knighted in 1785 solely to personal merit.

Most of the German settlers who rose to prominence in Quebec between 1760 and 1783 apparently entered Quebec with the British militias which had been recruited in New England. Among this group of Germans was the silversmith Johann Peter Arnoldi from the Mosel Valley (whose son Johann Daniel became famous as the "pioneer doctor of Lower Canada"); surveyor Peter Haldimand (nephew of Sir Frederick Haldimand); engineer and silversmith Joseph Schindler; Conrad Gugy (secretary to Haldimand and uncle of Louis Gugy); and furrier Thomas Wexler from Raab, Hungary (the first documented *Donauschwabe* in Canada). In the 1780's, several members of the Wurtele family are known to have immigrated to Quebec from the village of Strümpfelbach in Württemberg. One of their descendants, Justice J.C.S. Wurtele, was a politician, a Provincial Treasurer and the last Seigneur of Lower Canada in the second half of the 19th century. A few Germans, such as Swiss-born fur trader Lawrence Ermatinger, came as businessmen and as agents of London firms, hoping to benefit from the conquest of Quebec.

Some French-Canadian settlers of German descent trace their roots to the pre-1760 French army, which also included Germans. W.H. Debor lists some twenty-five such names traced in old Quebec marriage and baptismal registers. He also identified in mid-18th century New France a German fur trader by the name of Jean Joseph Hecker from the Diocese of Cologne. Virtually all of these Germans appear to have come from the German borderlands of France. French-Canadian chroniclers, according to Debor, indicated that Germans and their descendants retained their German identity in Quebec for a long time.

Settlers in 17th-century New France

Historical research since the mid-1950's has refuted the long-held assumption that only French Catholics immigrated to New France in the 17th century. We know now that prior to the revocation of the Edict of Nantes in 1685 not only French Protestants, but also non-French people -- Swiss, Scots, Irish, Germans, Basques, Italians, Jews, and New Englanders -- assimilated into the original French-Canadian society. Thanks to W.H. Debor's work, we have irrefutable evidence that natives of Germany lived in and around the city of Quebec as early as 1664, when New France counted a population of 2,000. The earliest known Germans -- Hans Bernhardt from the Mosel valley, Jean Daigre from Speyer, Hans Daigle from Vienna, and Joseph Brissac from Breisach -- could be identified because their purchase of property in Quebec or conversion to Roman Catholicism had been recorded. Their German ethnic identity must also have been noticeable because Daigle was given the nickname "Jean dit L'Allemand" and his grandchildren were still singled out as "L'Allemand."

Hans Daigle, whose descendants are numerous in Quebec today, had accompanied the French fur traders Radisson and Groseilliers to the Hudson Bay. The annexation of Alsace-Lorraine by France in 1648 may have brought German draftees from these regions to New France as early as 1665 to fight the Indians. Germans may also have come through the very active colony of German and Dutch Protestant merchants in early 17th-century Rouen, France. According to historian Jaenen, the French Crown ceded the administration of 17th-century New France to companies of entrepreneurs (usually Huguenot merchants from Dieppe and Rouen) who, in return for a trade monopoly, promised to settle the new lands. Another source of possible non-French immigration suggested by historian Brite, derived from France's rigourous policy throughout the 17th century of deporting criminals, vagrants, idlers, and all sorts of undesirables to New France.

Swiss-Canadian historians trace the origins of Swiss settlement back to the beginnings of Acadia. According to C.H. Bovay, a group of French Swiss or German Swiss soldiers in the service of the King of France were part of an expedition of 120 French under the Huguenot Monsieur de Monts who established a colony on the island of Sainte Croix (now Dochet Island) in Acadia in 1604. This was the first permanent settlement of Europeans in the New World north of Florida. On a sketch drawn by Samuel Champlain (who participated in this expedition) and published in 1613, one of the buildings in the colony is designated "logement des suisses." Because of an epidemic which killed 35 of the colonists, the colony was relocated to Port Royal in 1605, about 20 miles to the east on the Île Royal (now Cape Breton). There, another Swiss named Jean Vanuel (or Manuel) from Lucerne is known to have been employed as a tailor in 1638. Five years later, five young Swiss from the cantons of Fribourg, Lucerne, and Pays de Vaud were in the service of the Lieutenant Governor of Acadia. By the 1660's Swiss with German names such as Rotach and Steiner (or Steimer) are identifiable among the inhabitants of the town of Quebec and the Île d'Orléans facing it.

CHAPTER XXX

NEWFOUNDLAND

1. The community in the 19th and 20th centuries
2. Early migrations and contacts
3. Tyrkir and the Vinland Sagas

The community in the 19th and 20th centuries

Newfoundland along with Labrador was a separate Dominion until 1949. As Britain's oldest North American colony, it should come as no surprise that Germans visited it earlier than any other part of Canada. Many Germans came to Newfoundland by way of England, France, Canada, and the United States. The history of Newfoundland's German presence was shaped by this province's unique proximity to the world's richest fishing grounds and by the significance the fishery held for the economy, society, and culture of Newfoundland. From a mere seasonal fishing station with a migratory population in the 16th and 17th centuries, Newfoundland evolved into a flourishing maritime fish-trading centre in the 19th century, with a steadily growing population of permanent settlers, only to experience economic stagnation, relative overpopulation, and mass emigration in the 20th century. Its role as an exposed Allied base in two world wars against Germany and the chronic quest for revitalizing economic development have become two of the main issues affecting Newfoundland's Germans since World War I began.

Since Confederation with Canada in 1949, people of German origin have been Newfoundland's third largest non-native ethnic group after the British and the French. The present German community originated in the early 1950's when about one thousand German-speaking immigrants were attracted by the quest for industrialization and modernization. German entrepreneurs, professionals, and skilled workers started fifteen new industries in the 1950's and provided much required expertise.

Virtually no direct connections to Newfoundland's small pre-World War II community of Germans can be found today. As enemy aliens, Germans had been either interned or deported, or they left to avoid social ostracism in Newfoundland's tightly knit local fishing communities. Between the wars Germans were prominent largely in the brewing industry where German brewmasters were considered indispensable. Refugees from the Third Reich, an estimated 12,000 of whom pleaded for a haven from Nazi persecution, were refused admission prior to World War II. High unemployment and anti-foreign sentiment, created unfavourable conditions for immigration in general.

Prior to 1914, however, a sprinkling of Germans could be found among all walks of life, from seamen to entrepreneurs, entertainers, and teachers. Small identifiable German communities (numbering about 50 persons around 1900) existed in and around both the capital city of St. John's and the mining town of Betts Cove as well as at the Moravian mission stations in Labrador. However, Germans made their most significant contributions to the island as individual settlers, semi-permanent residents or visitors. In 1907, the Bavarian Otto Oppelt introduced professional wrestling to the island and was idolized by an entire generation of Newfoundlanders as the athlete "who could not be beaten." Newfoundland's national anthem, the Ode to Newfoundland, was first set to music by the German "Professor" E.R. Krippner in 1903. Ship engineer Robert von Stein, who married into one of the leading Newfoundland families, was called upon to resolve every imaginable engineering problem arising from the operation of Newfoundland's new railway, including the assembly of entire cars, in the 1880's and 1890's. Baron Francis von Ellershausen's spectacular exploitation of copper in Betts Cove in the 1870's turned Newfoundland into the world's sixth largest copper-producing country by 1880. In the second half of the 19th century Germans made an impact as entrepreneurs, physicians, engineers, teachers, watchmakers, jewellers, coopers, tailors, barbers, and gardeners.

Newfoundland had a burgeoning pre-World War I trade with Germany. It was instigated in the 1820's by Hamburg exporters using to their advantage the relaxation of the restrictions imposed by the British Navigation Acts of 1640-1660 on foreign shipping and trading with British colonies. The so-called Hamburg provisions trade from 1824 to 1870 introduced to Newfoundland German fishing equipment and German food staples, such as hard bread, butter, and meat, as well as music instruments, furniture, utensils, and machines of all kinds. Along with these came marketing and service personnel, as well as musicians and teachers. Newfoundland's demand for German provisions was such that Germany became Newfoundland's third largest importer in the 1850's. Most of the vessels carrying German cargo to Newfoundland were engaged in a triangular North Atlantic trade: they shipped Newfoundland saltfish to the West Indies and South America before returning from there via Europe. A number of Germans, such as importer James Christian Oelschläger and merchant-banker Albert Ehlers, who (like most British officials and professionals) did not establish a permanent residence on the island, nonetheless developed lasting business and family ties with Newfoundland.

Early migrations and contacts

In the 18th century, Germans are known to have come to Newfoundland as missionaries, soldiers, and refugees. The most eminent missionary of German descent was Swiss-born Lewis (Ludwig) Amadeus Anspach, whose grandfather was a native of the Palatinate. Anspach opened Newfoundland's first secondary school in 1798 where he himself taught. For twelve years he distinguished himself as an Anglican missionary, administrator of justice, and historian. Today a street bears his name in St. John's. Between 1752 and 1782, Moravian missionaries from Herrnhut in Saxony established three mission stations on the coast of Labrador (Nain, Okak, and Hopedale), which were occupied by German-speaking missionaries (see chapter XXVII). In 1762, Lieutenant Schuyler and about thirty of his German-American soldiers lost their lives in Newfoundland when their Royal American Regiment (composed of Germans and Swiss) was dispatched from New

York and Louisbourg to reconquer St. John's from the French. Between 1768 and 1819, two German physicians practised in Trinity, and the town's church registers for that period contain several other German names. The appointment of one John Ludwig as justice of the peace for Ferryland is documented for 1732. Of the 14,000 Palatine refugees who fled from Germany to London in 1709 in the hope of being taken to America (see chapter XXV, part 4), as many as five hundred are known to have been offered employment by English merchants engaged in the Newfoundland fisheries. How many actually came to the island is unknown.

In the 16th and 17th centuries, German names appear among the first French and British parties of colonists and explorers. Jean Decker, documented as a German baptized in Montreal in 1706, identified himself as born in Terreneuve in 1694 and married to a German woman. His parents appear to have been among the earliest known German settlers in the French colony of Placentia (started in 1657) or on Newfoundland's French Shore. Among Bonavista's inhabitants of 1698 was a fisherman named William Koch. Newfoundland's first planned English colony, started by John Guy in Cupids (Conception Bay) in 1610, included one trapper named "Fredrick the Dutchman," who may well have been a German. The first German whose presence in Newfoundland is documented beyond dispute was an "honest and religious" Saxon miner and ore expert named Daniel. Recruited for his expertise, he had accompanied Sir Humphrey Gilbert when the latter claimed the island for Queen Elizabeth in 1583. Daniel, to the delight of Gilbert, identified a variety of copper, iron, lead, and silver ores. Unfortunately, he drowned with his ores in a shipwreck before his return to Europe.

Evidence suggests that as early as the 16th century, German interest in Newfoundland was considerable and numerous contacts existed. Around 1600, Hamburg ships were known to have sailed to Newfoundland for cargoes of cod at the end of the fishing season. A German print portrayed the earliest picture of Inuit to Europeans. Three existing versions which circulated in Europe with text and dated 1566 show an Inuit woman and her child from Terra Nova. German cartographer Gerhard Mercator's world map of 1538 is the first map known to draw Newfoundland physically separate from Labrador.

We know that there has always been a community of Germans in England, many of them serving the country and its Royal House in wide-ranging capacities, such as mercenaries, merchants, artisans, and experts in mining and metallurgy. Therefore it is not surprising that German names appear in the earliest English records referring to Newfoundland. For example, a Master Grube from Plymouth was reported to have been in charge of two ships sent out in 1527 on one of the first recorded English voyages to Newfoundland.

Tyrkir and the Vinland sagas

The search for the first Germans to discover the New World has led some writers to two alleged German skippers, Didrik Pining and Hans Pothorst, in Danish service. They are supposed to have discovered Newfoundland on a mysterious expedition from Iceland more than two decades before John Cabot made his landfall. Whether, however, these two skippers visited Greenland, Labrador, or Newfoundland in 1472, 1476, or 1494 has not been verifiable.

The beginning of German associations with Newfoundland is lost in the mists of history, perhaps as remote as A.D. 1001, if we are to believe the Norwegian explorer Helge Ingstadt's contention that it was actually Leif Eirikson's legendary Norse expedition that landed in L'Anse aux Meadows in northern Newfoundland. Ingstadt has argued persuasively that this was the elusive Vinland, while other experts are considering it merely a Norse waystation to the true Vinland further south. Leif Eirikson, according to the Icelandic Sagas, was accompanied by a South German named Tyrkir. The sagas credit Tyrkir with discovering wild grapes at the landing site, hence suggesting the name of Vinland for the newly discovered land. The much debated question of whether grapes were actually found in northern Newfoundland seems to hinge on the credibility of Tyrkir who allegedly insisted that "I was born where there is no lack of either vines or grapes." Grapevines did not grow in Scandinavia and it has not been proven that they ever grew in Newfoundland. Either Tyrkir was a liar intent upon fooling his Norse companions or their friends back home, or he was, like so many a 20th-century German visitor, simply baffled by the abundance of berries as sweet and as large as grapes.

BIBLIOGRAPHY

This list contains the sources on which the individual chapters are based, as well as recommended additional reading.

CHAPTER I: GERMAN CANADIANS TODAY

Bassler, Gerhard P. "Germans in Canada: An Introduction to the Historiography," *The Immigration History Newsletter,* XX:1 (1988), 1-10.

Bassler, Gerhard P. "Problems and Perspectives in German-Canadian Historiography," *German-Canadian Studies Annals, 5 (1986), 1-19.*

Bassler, Gerhard P. "Silent or Silenced Co-founders of Canada? Reflections on the History of German Canadians," *Canadian Ethnic Studies,* XXII:1 (1990), 38-46.

Beutler, Bernhard A.H. "Deutschkanadischer Monat in Montreal," *German-Canadian Yearbook,* IV (1978), 312-314.

Bird, Michael and Terry Kobayashi. *A Splendid Harvest: Germanic Folk and Decorative Arts in Canada.* Toronto, 1981.

Cardinal, Clive H. von. "A German-Canadian Painter of Eskimo Life," *German-Canadian Yearbook,* 181-184.

Cardinal, Clive H. von. "Das kulturelle Leben der Kanadier deutscher und ukrainischer Herkunft," *German-Canadian Yearbook,* I (1973), 53-65.

Froeschle, Hartmut. "Eine Zentralstelle zur Erforschung deutschkanadischer Geschichte: Die 'Historical Society of Mecklenburg Upper Canada'," *German-Canadian Yearbook,* I (1973), 275-285.

Geiger-Torel, Hermann. "Canada, an Operatic Desert?" *German-Canadian Yearbook,* II (1975), 145-151.

Hiscock, Philip. "Tracing the origins of folk customs," *The Sunday Express* (St. John's, NF), 31 March 1991, 27.

Kallmann, Helmut. "The German Contribution to Music in Canada," *German-Canadian Yearbook,* II (1975), 152-166.

Lambton, Gunda. "Contributions of German Graphic Artists in the History of Canadian Printmaking," *German-Canadian Yearbook,* IV (1978), 180-204.

Panthel, Hans W. *With My Heart Half-Aglow: Impressions and Discourses in a German-Canadian Context.* Bochum 1991.

Riedel, Walter. "Der deutschkanadische Expressionist Herbert Siebner," *German-Canadian Yearbook,* VI (1981), 172-177.

Stabler, Hedy. "German Contributions to Our Heritage," *Saskatchewan Multicultural Magazine,* VI:4 (Fall 1985), 12-13.

Vincent, Dorothea. "Deutschkanadisches Geschäftsleben in Toronto zu Beginn der 70er Jahre," *German-Canadian Yearbook,* II (1975), 83-87.

Weimann, Gabriel and Conrad Winn. *The Zundel Affair, the Media, and Public Opinion in Canada.* Oakville, 1986

Zeidler, Eberhard A. "Architecture in Our Time--Necessities and Possibilities," *German-Canadian Yearbook,* IV (1978), 168-179.

CHAPTER II: THE GERMAN-CANADIAN MOSAIC

Amstatter, Andrew. *Tomslake: History of the Sudeten Germans in Canada.* Saanichton, B.C., 1978.

Becker, Anthony. "The Germans from Russia in Saskatchewan and Alberta," *German-Canadian Yearbook,* III (1976), 106-119.

Epp, Frank. "Mennonites in Canada," *German-Canadian Yearbook,* I (1973), 141-143.

Fry, Katharine Stenger. "The Danube Swabians in Canada: They Call it Their Land, too," *German-Canadian Yearbook,* VI (1981), 78-84.

Küster, Mathias. "Die Baltendeutschen in Kanada," *German-Canadian Yearbook,* V (1979), 55-65.

Lehmann, Heinz. *The German Canadians, 1750-1937: Immigration, Settlement and Culture.* St. John's, 1986.

Peters, Victor. "The Communal Settlements of the Hutterites in America," *German-Canadian Yearbook*, I (1973), 145-148.

Threinen, Norman J. "Lutherans in Canada," *German-Canadian Yearbook*, V (1979), 13-19.

CHAPTER III: THE ADJUSTMENT OF POST-WORLD WAR II IMMIGRANTS

Helling, Rudolf A. *A Socio-Economic History of German-Canadians: They, Too, Founded Canada.* Wiesbaden, 1984.

Kliem, Ottmar. "Deutsche in Kanada: Eine empirische Orientierungsstudie über den Integrationsprozess der Mitglieder des deutschen Klubs in Calgary, Alta. im Vergleich zu den Führern der deutschen Klubs in ganz Kanada." Ph.D. thesis, University of Erlangen-Nürnberg, 1969.

Leibbrandt, Gottlieb. "Deutschsprachiges Fernsehen in Kitchener-Waterloo," *German-Canadian Yearbook*, II (1975), 287-289.

Leibbrandt, Gottlieb. *Little Paradise: The Saga of the German Canadians of Waterloo County, Ontario, 1800 - 1975.* Kitchener, 1980.

Schindler, K.J. "Die deutschsprachigen katholischen Kirchengemeinden in Kanada--Teil 2," *German-Canadian Yearbook*, II (1975), 276-284.

Wekherlin, Robert P. "The German-Canadian Association of Alberta, Past and Present," *German-Canadian Yearbook*, IV (1978), 295-311.

Wieden, Fritz. *The Trans-Canada Alliance of German Canadians: A Study in Culture.* Windsor, Ont., 1985.

CHAPTER IV: THE IMMIGRATION OF THE 1950's

Bassler, Gerhard P. "Central European Immigrants in Post-Confederation St. John's, Newfoundland: Immigration and Adjustment," *Canadian Ethnic Studies / études ethniques au Canada,* XVIII:3 (1986), 37-46.

Bassler, Gerhard P. "'Develop or Perish': Joseph R. Smallwood and Newfoundland's Quest for German Industry," *Acadiensis,* XV:2 (1986), 93-119.

Broadfoot, Barry. *The Immigrant Years: From Europe to Canada, 1945 - 1967.* Vancouver/Toronto, 1986.

Bruce, Jean. *After the War.* Don Mills, 1982.

Green, Alan G. *Immigration and the Postwar Canadian Economy.* Toronto, 1976.

Richmond, Anthony H. *Post-War Immigrants in Canada.* Toronto, 1967.

Whitaker, Reg. *The Secret History of Canadian Immigration.* Toronto, 1988.

CHAPTER V: ADMISSION OF REFUGEES AND DISPLACED PERSONS 1945-1950

Bassler, Gerhard P. "Canadian Postwar Immigration Policy and the Admission of German Enemy Aliens, 1945-50," *Yearbook of German-American Studies,* 22 (1987), 183-197.

Bassler, Gerhard P. "German Immigration to Canada 1945-1950: Issues and Questions," *German-Canadian Studies Annals,* 6 (1988), 168-179.

Bruce, Jean. *After the War.* Don Mills, 1982.

Dirks, Gerald E. *Canada's Refugee Policy: Indifference or Opportunism?* Montreal, 1977.

Epp, Frank H. *Mennonite Exodus: The Rescue and Resettlement of the Russian Mennonites since the Communist Revolution.* Altona, Man., 1962.

Hawkins, Freda. *Canada and Immigration: Public Policy and Public Concern.* Montreal, 1972.

Keyserlingk, Robert Wendelin. *Unfinished History.* London, 1948.

Küster, Mathias. "Die Baltendeutschen in Kanada," *German-Canadian Yearbook,* V (1979), 55-65.

Sturhahn, William J.H. "Bemerkungen über die Einwanderung deutscher Baptisten nach dem Zweiten Weltkrieg," *German-Canadian Yearbook,* IV (1978), 122-126.
Sturhahn, William J.H. *They Came From East and West: A History of Immigration to Canada.* Winnipeg, 1976.

CHAPTER VI: ORIGINS OF THE POST-WORLD WAR II IMMIGRATION

Benz, Wolfgang, ed. *Die Vertreibung der Deutschen aus dem Osten: Ursachen, Ereignisse, Folgen.* Frankfurt a. M., 1985.

Buchsweiler, Meir. *Volksdeutsche in der Ukraine am Vorabend und Beginn des Zweiten Weltkriegs: ein Fall doppelter Loyalität?* Gerlingen, 1984.

Clay, Luicius D. *Decision in Germany.* New York, 1950.

Dallin, Alexander. *German Rule in Russia, 1941 - 1945: A Study of Occupation Policies.* Boulder, Colo., 1981.

de Zayas, Alfred M. *Nemesis at Potsdam: The Anglo-Americans and the Expulsion of the Germans: Background, Execution, Consequences.* London, 1977.

Fleischhauer, Ingeborg. *Das Dritte Reich und die Deutschen in der Sowjetunion.* Stuttgart, 1983.

Fleischhauer, Ingeborg and Benjamin Pinkus. *The Soviet Germans, Past and Present.* London, 1986.

Keyserlingk, Robert H. *Austria in World War II: An Anglo-American Dilemma.* Kingston and Montréal, 1988.

Kulischer, Eugene M. *The Displacement of Population in Europe.,* Montréal, 1943.

Kulischer, Eugene M. *Europe on the Move: War and Population Changes, 1917 - 1947.* New York, 1948.

Schechtman, Joseph B. *European Population Transfers, 1939 - 1945.* New York, 1946.

Sheehy, Ann. *The Crimean Tartars, Volga Germans and Meskhetians: Soviet Treatment of Some National Minorities.* London, 1973.

CHAPTER VII: THE WORLD WAR II EXPERIENCE IN CANADA

Bassler, Gerhard P. "The Enemy Within: The World War II Experience of German Immigrants in Canada, 1939-1941," paper presented to World War II Conference, Siena College, 1989.

Carter, David J. *Behind Canadian Barbed Wire: Alien and German Prisoners of War Camps in Canada, 1914 - 1946.* Calgary, 1980.

Draper, Paula Jean. "The Accidental Immigrants: Canada and the Interned Refugees," *Canadian Jewish Historical Society Journal,* X:1 and 2 (1978), 1-38, 80-112.

Jong, Louis de. *The German Fifth Column in the Second World War.* Chicago, 1956.

Kelly, John Joseph. "The Prisoner of War Camps in Canada, 1939-1947," M.A. thesis, University of Windsor, 1976.

Keyserlingk, Robert H. "Agents Within the Gates: The Search For Nazi Subversives in Canada During World War II," *Canadian Historical Review,* 66 (1985), 211-239.

Keyserlingk, Robert H. "The Canadian Government's Attitude Towards German Canadians in WW II," *Canadian Ethnic Studies,* 14 (1984), 16-29.

Keyserlingk, Robert H. "Which Fatherland in War? The Canadian Government's View of German-Canadian Loyalties in World War Two," in T. Yedlin, ed. *Central and East European Ethnicity in Canada: Adaptation and Preservation.* Edmonton, 1985.

Melady, John. *Escape from Canada! The Untold Story of German POW's in Canada, 1939 - 1945.* Toronto, 1981.

CHAPTER VIII: BETWEEN THE WORLD WARS

Avery, Donald. *'Dangerous Foreigners:' European Immigrant Workers and Labour Radicalism in Canada, 1896 - 1932.* Toronto, 1979.

Bassler, Gerhard P. "Franz Straubinger and the Deutsche Arbeitsgemeinschaft Ontario," *German-Canadian Yearbook,* VIII (1984), 225-235.

Eayrs, James. *In Defence of Canada.* Toronto, 1965.

England, Robert. *The Central European Immigrant in Canada.* Toronto, 1929.

England, Robert. *The Colonization of Western Canada: A Study of Contemporary Land Settlement (1896-1934).* London, 1936.

Epp, Frank H. *Mennonites in Canada, 1920-1940: A People's Struggle for Survival.* Toronto, 1982.

Grossmann, John. "Streiflichter vom Rande der Zivilisation: Die Erlebnisse eines deutschen Heimstätters im Peace River-Gebiet--Parts 1 and 2," *German-Canadian Yearbook,* I (1973), 191-244, and II (1975), 193-246.

Jones, Thomas. *Lloyd George.* Cambridge, Mass., 1951.

Keyserlingk, Robert H. "A Case of Cultural Proximity: Canadian Prime Minister Mackenzie King and Hitler," *German-Canadian Studies Annals,* 6 (1988), 154-167.

Kuester, Mathias F. "Die Deutschen Tage -- ein historischer Rückblick," in German-Canadian Association of Alberta, ed. *Deutsche Tage 1987,* Edmonton, 1987, 12-14.

Lehmann, Heinz. *The German Canadians, 1750-1937: Immigration, Settlement and Culture.* St. John's, 1986.

Leibbrandt, Gottlieb. *Little Paradise: The Saga of the German Canadians of Waterloo County, Ontario, 1800-1975.* Kitchener, 1980.

McNaught, Kenneth. *The Pelican History of Canada.* Harmondsworth, 1969.

Palmer, Howard. *Patterns of Prejudice: A History of Nativism in Alberta.* Toronto, 1982.

Rothfels, Hans. *The German Opposition to Hitler: An Appraisal.* Chicago, 1962.

Teatero, William. *Mackenzie King: Man of Mission.* Toronto, 1979.

Wagner, Jonathan F. *Brothers Beyond the Sea: National Socialism in Canada.* Waterloo, Ont., 1981.

Wagner, Jonathan F. "Transferred Crisis: German Volkish Thought Among Russian Mennonite Immigrants to Western Canada," *Canadian Review of Studies in Nationalism,* I (1974), 202-220.

CHAPTER IX: REFUGEES FROM THE THIRD REICH

Abella, Irving and Harold Troper. "The German-Jewish Intellectual and Canadian Immigration, 1933-1945," *German-Canadian Studies Annals,* 4 (1983), 167-184.

Abella, Irving and Harold Troper. *None Is Too Many: Canada and the Jews of Europe, 1933-1948.* Toronto, 1983.

Amstatter, Andrew. *Tomslake: History of the Sudeten Germans in Canada.* Saanichton, B.C., 1978.

Bassler, Gerhard P. "Attempts to Settle Jewish Refugees in Newfoundland and Labrador, 1934-1939," *Simon Wiesenthal Center Annual,* 5 (1988), 121-144.

Bassler, Gerhard P. "Newfoundland and Refugees from the Third Reich, 1933-1941," *Newfoundland Studies,* III:1 (Spring 1987), 37-70.

Bassler, Gerhard P. "Newfoundland's 'Dangerous' Internees Who Never Were: The History of Victoria Camp, Carbonear, 1940-1943," *Newfoundland Studies,* V:1 (1989), 39-51.

Bassler, Gerhard P. *Sanctuary Denied: Refugees from the Third Reich and Newfoundland Immigration Policy, 1906-1949.* St. John's, 1992.

Gürttler, Karin. "Exilschriftsteller in Kanada." Unpublished manuscript, 1978.

Gow, B.A. "A Home for Free Germans in the Wilderness of Canada: The Sudeten German Settlers of Tupper Creek, B.C.," *Canadian Ethnic Studies,* X:1 (1978), 62-74.

Jong, Louis de. *The German Fifth Column in the Second World War.* Chicago, 1956.

Kastens, Eva. "Botschafter im Arbeitskleid -- Aus der Geschichte der Sudetendeutschen in Kanada," *German-Canadian Yearbook,* III (1976), 120-128.

Koch, Eric. *Deemed Suspect: A Wartime Blunder.* Agincourt, 1980.

Kochan, Miriam. *Britain's Internees in the Second World War.* London and Basingstoke, 1983.

Rosenberg, Louis. *Canada's Jews: A Social and Economic Study of the Jews in Canada.* Montreal, 1939.

Wanka, Willi. *Opfer des Friedens: Die Sudetensiedlungen in Kanada.* München, 1988.

Wanka, Willi. "Tomslake 1939: The Sudeten Story," in Lillian York, ed., *Lure of the South Peace: Tales of the Early Pioneers to 1945.* South Peace, 1981.

Wieden, Fritz. *Kanadas Sudetendeutsche.* Stuttgart, 1984.

CHAPTER X: IMMIGRATION FROM GERMANY BETWEEN THE WORLD WARS

Bassler, Gerhard P. "German Overseas Migration to North America in the Nineteenth and Twentieth Centuries: Recent German Research from a Canadian Perspective," *German-Canadian Yearbook,* VII (1983), 8-21.

Bickelmann, Hartmut. *Deutsche Überseeauswanderung in der Weimarer Zeit.* Wiesbaden, 1980.

Gossner, Ewald. *Blood, Sweat and Tears: A Biography.* Battleford, 1986.

Grossmann, John. "Streiflichter vom Rande der Zivilisation, Teil 1: Die Erlebnisse eines deutschen Heimstätters im Peace River-Gebiet," *German-Canadian Yearbook,* I (1973), 191-244.

Hedges, James B. *Building the Canadian West: The Land and Colonization Policy of the Canadian Pacific Railway.* New York, 1939.

Labudde, Hans-Jürgen. "Die deutsche Auswanderung nach Kanada," Ph.D. thesis, University of Hamburg, 1952.

Lehmann, Heinz. *The German Canadians, 1750-1937: Immigration, Settlement and Culture.* St. John's, 1986.

Wagner, Hermann. "Kanada und die deutscheAuswanderung," *Zeitwende,* VI (1930), 385-395.

Wagner, Hermann. *Von Küste zu Küste: Bei deutschen Auswanderern in Kanada.* Hamburg, 1929.

Wagner, Jonathan, ed. "Baronin Dr. Edith von Schilling: Deutsche Siedler in Nord-Saskatchewan," *German-Canadian Yearbook,* IV (1978), 257-265.

CHAPTER XI: IMMIGRATION FROM CENTRAL AND EASTERN EUROPE

Epp, Frank H. *Mennonites in Canada, 1920-1940: A People's Struggle for Survival.* Toronto, 1982.

Epp, Frank H. *Mennonite Exodus: The Rescue and Resettlement of the Russian Mennonites since the Communist Revolution.* Altona, Man., 1962.

Francis, E.K. *In Search of Utopia: The Mennonites of Manitoba.* Altona, Man., 1955.

Koch, Fred C. *The Volga Germans: In Russia and the Americas, from 1763 to the Present.* University Park, Pa., 1977.

Lehmann, Heinz. *The German Canadians, 1750-1937: Immigration, Settlement and Culture.* St. John's, 1986.

Toews, John B. *Lost Fatherland: The Story of the Mennonite Emigration from Soviet Russia, 1921-1927.* Scottdale, Pa., 1967.

Wagner, Jonathan F. "Transferred Crisis: German Volkish Thought Among Russian Mennonite Immigrants to Western Canada," *Canadian Review of Studies in Nationalism,* I:2 (1974), 202-220.

CHAPTER XII: THE HUTTERITES

Bennett, John W. *Hutterian Brethren: The Agricultural Economy and Social Organization of a Communal People.* Stanford, 1967.

Brednich, Rolf Wilhelm. *The Bible and the Plow: The Lives of a Hutterite Minister and a Mennonite Farmer.* Ottawa, 1981.

Flint, David. *The Hutterites: A Study in Prejudice.* Toronto, 1975.

Holzach, Michael. *Das vergessene Volk: Ein Jahr bei den deutschen Hutterern in Canada.* Hamburg, 1980.

Horsch, John. *The Hutterite Brethren, 1528-1931: A Story of Martyrdom and Loyalty.* Cayley, Alta., 1977.

Hostetler, John A. *Hutterite Society.* Baltimore, 1974.

Hostetler, John A. and Gertrude Enders Huntingdon. *The Hutterites in North America.* New York, 1967.

Längin, Bernd G. *Die Hutterer: Gefangene der Vergangenheit, Pilger der Gegenwart, Propheten der Zukunft.* Hamburg, 1986.

Nikiforuk, Andrew. "Community Life," *Equinox,* May/June 1987, 24-35.

Peter, Karl. *The Dynamics of Hutterite Society: An Analytical Approach.* Edmonton, 1986.

Peters, Victor. *All Things Common: The Hutterian Way of Life.* Minneapolis, 1965.

Ryan, John. *The Agricultural Economy of Manitoba Hutterite Colonies.* Ottawa, 1977.

Wollman, Ruth J. "Hutterite History and Customs," *Saskatchewan Multicultural Magazine,* V:1 (Winter 1985/86), 8-9.

CHAPTER XIII: THE WORLD WAR I EXPERIENCE

Avery, Donald. *Dangerous Foreigners:' European Immigrant Workers and Labour Radicalism in Canada, 1896-1932.* Toronto, 1979.

Bassler, Gerhard P. "The Enemy Alien Experience in Newfoundland, 1914-1918," *Canadian Ethnic Studies / études ethniques au Canada,* XX:3 (1988), 42-62.

Bausenhart, Werner A. "The Ontario German Language Press and its Suppression by Order-in-Council in 1918," *Canadian Ethnic Studies / études ethniques au Canada,* IV:1/2 (1972), 35-48.

Boudreau, J.A. "Western Canada's Enemy Aliens in World War One," *Alberta History,* XII:1 (1964), 1-9.

Bridgman, Reverend Wellington. *Breaking Prairie Sod.* Toronto, 1920.

Entz, W. "The Suppression of the German Language Press in September 1918 (with special reference to the secular German language press in western Canada)" *Canadian Ethnic Studies / études ethniques au Canada,* VIII:2 (1976), 56-70.

English, John and Kenneth McLaughlin, ed. *Kitchener: An Illustrated History.* Waterloo, 1983.

Friesen, Gerhard. "The Presentation of German-Canadian Concerns in the *Berliner Journal,* 1914-1917," *German-Canadian Studies Annals,* 6 (1988), 138-153.

Grenke, Art. "The German Community of Winnipeg and the English-Canadian Response to World War I," *Canadian Ethnic Studies,* XX:1 (1988), 21-44.

Lee-Whiting, Brenda. "'Enemy Aliens': German-Canadians on the Home Front," *The Beaver,* 69:5 (October-November 1989), 53-58.

Leibbrandt, G. *Little Paradise: The Saga of the German Canadians of Waterloo County, Ontario, 1800-1975.* Kitchener, 1980.

McKegney, Patricia P. *The Kaiser's Bust: A Study of Wartime Propaganda in Berlin, Ontario, 1914-1918.* Bamberg, Ontario, 1991.

Morton, Desmond. *The Canadian General Sir William Otter.* Toronto, 1974.

Morton, Desmond. "Sir William Otter and Internment Operations in Canada during the First World War," *Canadian Historical Review,* LV:1 (1974), 32-58.

Mulvey, Thomas. "Our Alien Enemies," *The Canadian Magazine,* XLIV:2 (December 1914), 137-140.

Palmer, Howard. *Patterns of Prejudice: A History of Nativism in Alberta.* Toronto, 1982.

Thompson, John Herd. *The Harvests of War: The Prairie West, 1914-1918.* Toronto, 1978.

Wilson, Barbara M., ed. *Ontario and the First World War, 1914-1918.* Toronto, 1977.

CHAPTER XIV: ON THE EVE OF WORLD WAR I

Canada, Parliament. *Official Report of the Debates of the House of Commons,* Fourth Session, Tenth Parliament, 1907-8. Ottawa, 1907-8, 6825-6834.

Crowfoot, A.H. *This Dream: Life of Isaac Hellmuth.* Toronto, 1963.

Dunham, Mabel. *Grand River.* Toronto, 1945.

Entz, Werner. "Der Einfluss der deutschsprachigen Presse Westkanadas auf die Organisationsbestrebungen des dortigen Deutschtums, 1889-1939," *German-Canadian Yearbook,* II (1975), 92-138.

Helling, Rudolf A. *A Socio-Economic History of German-Canadians: They, Too, Founded Canada.* Wiesbaden, 1984.

Kalbfleisch, Herbert Karl. *The History of the Pioneer German Language Press of Ontario, 1835-1918.* Toronto, 1968.

Lehmann, Heinz. *The German Canadians, 1750-1937: Immigration, Settlement and Culture.* St. John's, 1986.

Leibbrandt, G. *Little Paradise: The Saga of the German Canadians of Waterloo County, Ontario, 1800-1975.* Kitchener, 1980.

Maron, Gotthard L. *Facts about the Germans in Canada.* Winnipeg, 1914.

Miller, H.H. "Die Deutschen in Canada," *Deutsch-Amerikanische Geschichtsblätter,* 8 (1908), 118-124.

Woodworth, James S. *Strangers Within Our Gates: Or Coming Canadians.* Toronto, 1909.

CHAPTER XV: PIONEERS IN BRITISH COLUMBIA

Hansen, Marcus Lee. *The Atlantic Migration, 1607-1860: A History of the Continuing Settlement of the United States.* New York, 1961.

Laue, Ingrid E. "Gustav Konstantin Alvo von Alvensleben (1879-1965): Ein Lebensbild," *German-Canadian Yearbook,* V (1979), 154-173.

Liddell, Peter. "The First Germans in British Columbia?" *German-Canadian Yearbook,* VI (1981), 74-77.

Liddell, Peter. "Germans on Canada's Pacific Slopes: A Brief Survey of German Discovery, Settlement and Culture in British Columbia, 1778 to the Present," *Yearbook of German-American Studies,* XVI (1981), 51-58.

Liddell, Peter. "With so many trees, where is the forest?"- on the History of the Germans in British Columbia," *German Canadian Studies Annals,* 3 (1980), 102-105.

Mayer, Elizabeth M. *Stories About People of German-Language Background in Victoria, B.C.: As They Lived Within the Framework of Canadian and German History Between 1850 and 1985.* Victoria, 1986.

Nagler, Joerg A. "Enemy Aliens and Internment in World War I: Alvo von Alversleben in Fort Douglas, Utah, a Case Study," *Utah Historical Quarterly,* 58 (1990), 387-405.

Ramsay, Bruce. *A History of the German-Canadians in British Columbia.* Vancouver, 1958.

Riedel, Walter E. "John Sebastian Helmcken: Pioneer Surgeon and Legislator (1824-1920)," *German-Canadian Yearbook,* IV (1978), 250-256.

Smith, Dorothy Blakey, ed. *The Reminiscences of Dr. John Sebastian Helmcken.* Vancouver, 1975.

CHAPTER XVI: PIONEERS IN ALBERTA

Cardinal, Clive H. "A Note on Martin Nordegg (1868-1948)," *German-Canadian Yearbook,* IV (1978), 246-249.

Eberhard, Elvire. "The Growth of the German Population in Medicine Hat, Alta.," *German-Canadian Yearbook,* VI (1981), 62-65.

Entz, Werner. "Alfred Freiherr von Hammerstein -- ein deutschkanadischer Pionier," *Toronto Courier,* December 13, 1973.

Gerwin, Elizabeth B. "A Survey of the German-speaking Population of Alberta," M.A. thesis, University of Alberta,1938.

Herzer, John E. *Homesteading for God: A Narrative History of Lutheran Mission Work in Alberta and British Columbia, 1894-1946.* Edmonton, 1946.

Lehmann, Heinz. *The German Canadians, 1750-1937: Immigration, Settlement and Culture.* St. John's, 1986.

Malycky, Alexander. "The German-Albertans. A Bibliography. Parts 1 and 2," *German-Canadian Yearbook,* VI (1981), 311-344; VII (1983), 239-325.

Nordegg, Martin. *The Possibilities of Canada Are Truly Great: Memoirs 1906-1924.* Toronto, 1971.

Palmer, Howard. *Patterns of Prejudice: A History of Nativism in Alberta.* Toronto, 1982.

Palmer, Howard and Tamara, eds. *Peoples of Alberta: Portraits of Cultural Diversity.* Saskatoon, 1985.

Yedlin, Y., ed. *Germans from Russia in Alberta:Reminiscences.* Edmonton, 1984.

CHAPTER XVII: PIONEERS IN SASKAT-CHEWAN

Epp, Frank H. *Mennonites in Canada, 1786-1920: the History of a Separate People.* Toronto, 1974.

Holdfast History and Heritage Committee, comp. *Holdfast: History and Heritage.* Holdfast, 1980.

Klaassen, H.T. *Birth and Growth of the Eigenheim Mennonite Church, 1892-1974.* Rosthern, [1974?].

Lehmann, Heinz. *The German Canadians, 1750-1937: Immigration, Settlement and Culture.* St. John's, 1986.

Lizee, Simon, ed. *A Cross in the Clearing: A History of Annaheim and District, 1902-1980.* Melfort, Sask., 1980.

Lutz, Otto. *A Mother Braving a Wilderness: Told by her Son, Otto Lutz.* Muenster, 1977.

Meilicke, E.J. *Leaves from the Life of a Pioneer: Being the Autobiography of Sometime Senator Emil Julius Meilicke.* Vancouver, 1949.

Metzger, H. "Historical Sketch of St. Peter's Parish and the Founding of the Colonies of Rastatt, Katharinenthal and Speyer," *Saskatchewan Genealogical Society Bulletin,* V:4 (1974), 7-29.

N.A. *Souvenir of the Silver Jubilee of St. Peter's Colony, 1903-1928.* Muenster, Sask., 1928.

Plemel, Sister Benedict. *Sail On: Ursuline Convent 1913-1973 Diamond Jubilee.* Bruno, Sask., 1973.

Renneberg, Werner, ed. *Homesteading to Homecoming, 1903-1971: A History of St. Gregor and District.* Muenster, Sask., 1971.

[Schulte, W., ed.] *Pictures and Pages on the Silver Jubilee of St. Joseph's Colony, compiled by the Oblate Priests in the Colony.* Translated by Lambert and Tilly Schneider. Saskatoon, [1986?].

Tischler, Kurt. "The German Canadians in Saskatchewan, with Particular Reference to the Language Problem,1900-1930," M.A. thesis, University of Saskatchewan, 1978.

Windschiegl, Peter. *Fifty Golden Years, 1903-1953: A Brief History of the Order of St. Benedict in the Abbacy Nullius of St. Peter, Muenster, Saskatchewan.* Muenster, Sask., 1953.

Zarek, E.H. and C.R. Hennings. "Zur Geschichte der Siedlung Edenwald," *Deutschtum im Ausland* (Stuttgart), XVIII:3 (1934), 148-156.

CHAPTER XVIII: PIONEERS IN MANITOBA

Entz, Werner. "Ein Deutscher in Manitoba," *Toronto Courier,* January 6, 1972.

Entz, Werner. "William Hespeler, Manitoba's First German Consul," *German-Canadian Yearbook,* I (1973), 149-152.

Epp, Frank H. *Mennonites in Canada, 1786-1920: The History of a Separate People.* Toronto, 1974.

Francis, E.K. *In Search of Utopia: The Mennonites in Manitoba.* Altona, 1955.

Friesen, J. et al, eds. *Grunthal History, 1874-1974.* Grunthal, 1974.

Gerbrandt, H.J. *Adventure in Faith: the Background in Europe and the Development in Canada of the Bergthaler Mennonite Church of Manitoba.* Altona, Man., 1970.

Grenke, Arthur. "The Formation and Early Development of an Urban Ethnic Community: A Case Study of the Germans in Winnipeg, 1872-1919," Ph.D. thesis, University of Manitoba, 1975.

Gürttler, Karin. "Das Manitoba-Siedlungsprojekt der Deutschen Gesellschaft zu Montreal," *German-Canadian Yearbook,* X (1988), 33-71.

Klippenstein, L. and J.G. Toews, eds. *Mennonite Memories: Settling in Western Canada.* Winnipeg, 1977.

Lehmann, Heinz. *The German Canadians, 1750-1937: Immigration, Settlement and Culture.* St. John's, 1986.

Manitoba Library Association, ed. *Pioneers and Early Citizens of Manitoba.* Winnipeg, 1972.

Smith, C. Henry. *The Coming of the Russian Mennonites.* Berne, Ind., 1927.

Warkentin, A. *Reflections on Our Heritage: A History of Steinbach and the R.M. of Hanover from 1874.* Steinbach, Man., 1974.

CHAPTER XIX: ROOTS OF THE WESTERN CANADIAN PIONEERS

Baden-Württemberg, Innenministerium, ed. *Die Donauschwaben: Deutsche Siedlung in Osteuropa.* Sigmaringen, 1987.

Chmelnar, Johann. "The Austrian Emigration, 1900-1914," in D. Fleming and B. Bailyn, eds. *Perspectives in American History,* vol. VII. Cambridge, Mass., 1974, 275-378.

Giesinger, Adam. *From Catherine to Khrushchev: The Story of Russia's Germans.* Winnipeg, 1974.

Koch, Fred C. *The Volga Germans in Russia and the Americas, From 1763 to the Present.* University Park and London, 1977.

Lehmann, Heinz. *The German Canadians, 1750-1937: Immigration, Settlement and Culture.* St. John's, 1986.

Sallet, Richard. *Russian-German Settlements in the United States.* Fargo, 1974.

Troper, Harold. *Only Farmers Need Apply: Official Canadian Government Encouragement of Immigration from the United States, 1896-1911.* Toronto, 1972.

Williams, Hattie Plum. *The Czar's Germans, With Particular Reference to the Volga Germans.* Lincoln, 1975.

Zöllner, Erich. *Geschichte Österreichs: Von den Anfängen bis zur Gegenwart.* Wien, 1970.

CHAPTER XX: GERMANS IN PRE-CONFEDERATION CANADA

Cronmiller, Carl R. *A. History of the Lutheran Church in Canada.* Vol. I. Toronto, 1961.

Debor, H.W. *1664-1964: Die Deutschen in der Provinz Quebec.* Montreal, 1963.

Debor, H.W. "Pionier der kanadischen Seefahrt: Wilhelm Munderloh schuf Dampfschiff-Verbindung zwischen Canada und Europa," *Toronto Courier,* [?].

Debor, H.W. "Sie kamen nicht mit leeren Händen...: Der kulturelle Beitrag der ersten deutschen Einwanderer und ihrer Nachkommen im Osten Kanadas," *Manitoba Courier,* Februar 16, 1961.

Gerhard, Karl. *100 Jahre Johannesgemeinde Montreal.* Montreal, 1953.

German Society, Montreal, ed. *German Canadian Artists in Québec.* Montreal, 1985.

Gürttler, Karin R. *Geschichte der Deutschen Gesellschaft zu Montreal, 1835-1985.* Montreal, 1985.

Johnson, J.K. "Zimmerman, Samuel," *Dictionary of Canadian Biography,* VIII (1985).

Josephy, Alvin M. *The Artist was a Young Man: The Life Story of Peter Rindisbacher.* Fort Worth, 1970.

Kallmann, Helmut. "The German Contribution to Music in Canada," *German-Canadian Yearbook,* II (1975), 152-166.

Kallmann, Helmut. "Nordheimer, Abraham," *Dictionary of Canadian Biography,* Vol. IX (1976).

Lach, Friedhelm. "Deutschkanadische Kunst in Québec," *Annalen Deutschkanadische Studien,* 5 (1986), 125-132.

Möllmann, Albert. *Das Deutschtum in Montreal.* Jena, 1937.

Rapp, Eugen. "180 Jahre deutsche Siedlung in Hamilton: Eine Zeittafel der deutschen Einwanderungsgeschichte (II)," *Courier,* January 15, 1970.

Reid, Dennis. *Our Own Country Canada: Being an Account of the National Aspirations of the Principal Landscape Artists in Montreal and Toronto, 1860-1890.* Ottawa, 1979.

Weissenborn, Georg K. "Johann Daniel Arnoldi: The Pioneer Doctor of Lower Canada (1774-1849)," *German-Canadian Yearbook,* IV (1978), 254-256.

"Württemberger standen an der Wiege der Deutschen Gesellschaft Montreal: Eine Betrachtung aus Anlass des Jahresballes der Deutschen Gesellschaft," *Montreal Courier,* January 25, 1962.

CHAPTER XXI: DESTINATION OTTAWA VALLEY

Bausenhart, Werner. "The German Settlement of Ladysmith, Quebec, and the Dialect Spoken by its Settlers," *German-Canadian Yearbook,* IV (1978), 234-245.

Hessel, Peter. *Destination: Ottawa Valley.* Ottawa, 1984.

Hessel, Peter. "German Immigration to the Ottawa Valley in the 19th Century," *German-Canadian Yearbook,* VIII (1984), 67-94.

Kuntz, Edith. "Alte deutsche Siedlung Ladysmith," *Kanada Kurier,* December 1, 1983.

Lee-Whiting, Brenda. *Harvest of Stones: The German Settlement in Renfrew County.* Toronto, 1985.

Lee-Whiting, Brenda. *On Stony Ground.* Renfrew, 1986.

Lee-Whiting, Brenda. "The Opeongo Road -- An early Settlement Scheme," *Canadian Geographical Journal,* 74 (1967), 76-83.

Lee-Whiting, Brenda. "Why So Many German Immigrants Embarked at Liverpool," *German-Canadian Yearbook,* IX (1986), 71-79.

Lewis, Gertrud Jaron. "The German Presence in the Ontario Northland," *German-Canadian Yearbook,* VIII (1984), 24-66.

St. John's Lutheran Church, Bonnechere, Ontario. *1863-1988: 125th Anniversary.* Bonnechere, 1988.

Wagner, W. *Canada, ein Land für deutsche Auswanderung.* Berlin, 1961.

Zion Lutheran Church, Augsburg (Ont.). *Zion Augsburg: 110 Anniversary, 1874-1984.* Augsburg (Ont.), 1984.

CHAPTER XXII: LITTLE GERMANY IN WATERLOO COUNTY

English, John and Kenneth McLaughlin. *Kitchener: An Illustrated History.* Waterloo, 1983.

Hess, Anna K. "Die Deutschen in Kanada," in German Canadian Alliance, ed. *Festschrift zur Zweihundert-Jahrfeier deutscher Siedlung in Kanada, 1752-1952.* Toronto, 1952, 7-25.

Kalbfleisch, Herbert Karl. *The History of the Pioneer German Language Press of Ontario, 1835-1918.* Toronto, 1968.

Leibbrandt, Gottlieb. "Deutsche Ortsgründungen und Ortsnamen in der Graftschaft Waterloo," *German-Canadian Yearbook,* I (1973), 119-130.

Leibbrandt, Gottlieb. "100 Jahre Concordia," *German-Canadian Yearbook,* I (1973), 263-274.

Leibbrandt, Gottlieb. *Little Paradise: The Saga of the German Canadians of Waterloo County, Ontario, 1800-1975.* Kitchener, 1980.

McKegney, Patricia Pearl. "The German Schools of Waterloo County, 1851-1930," *Waterloo Historical Society, Annual Report,* 58 (1970), 54-67.

Moyer, Bill. *Kitchener Yesterday Revisited: An Illustrated History.* Burlington, Ont., 1979.

Moyer, Bill. *This Unique Heritage: The Story of Waterloo County.* Kitchener, 1971.

Moyer, William G. "The Early Days in Waterloo County," *German-Canadian Yearbook,* I (1973), 113-118.

Seidenfaden, Marie-Louise. *"...wir ziehen nach Amerika: " Briefe Odenwälder Auswanderer aus den Jahren 1830-1833.* Schloß Lichtenberg, 1986.

CHAPTER XXIII: FIRST MASS EXODUS FROM GERMANY TO CANADA

Andre, John. *Infant Toronto as Simcoe's Folly.* Toronto, 1971.

Andre, John. *William Berczy, Co-Founder of Toronto.* Toronto, 1967.

Arndt, Karl J.R. "The Peter Rindisbacher Family on the Red River in Rupert's Land: Their Hardships and Call for Help from Rapp's Harmony Society," *German-Canadian Yearbook,* I (1973), 95-106.

Bassler, Gerhard P. "Die Anfänge der deutschen Massenwanderung nach Britisch Nordamerika im 19. Jahrhundert," *Annalen Deutschkanadische Studien,* 2 (1978), 4-18.

Bassler, Gerhard. "Auswanderungsfreiheit und Auswandererfürsorge in Württemberg, 1815-1855: Zur Geschichte der südwestdeutschen Massenwanderung nach Nordamerika," *Zeitschrift für württembergische Landesgeschichte,* XXXIII (1974), 117-160.

Bassler, Gerhard. "The 'Inundation' of British North America with 'the Refuse of Foreign Pauperism:' Assisted Emigration from Southern Germany in the mid-19th Century," *German-Canadian Yearbook,* IV (1978), 93-113.

Beringer, Walter. "A Leader and His People. Scenes from the Life of Albrecht Ulrich Moll alias William Berczy (1744-1813)," *German-Canadian Yearbook,* VIII (1984), 95-114.

Dunham, Mabel. *Grand River.* Toronto, 1945.

Hansen, Marcus Lee and J.B. Brebner. *The Mingling of the Canadian and American Peoples. Vol. I: Historical.* Toronto, 1940.

Hippel, Wolfgang von. *Auswanderung aus Südwestdeutschland: Studien zur württembergischen Auswanderung und Auswanderungspolitik im 18. und 19. Jahrhundert.* Stuttgart, 1984.

Lehmann, Heinz. *The German Canadians, 1750-1937: Immigration, Settlement and Culture.* St. John's, 1986.

Marschalck, Peter. *Deutsche Überseewanderung im 19. Jahrhundert: Ein Beitrag zu soziologischen Theorie der Bevölkerung.* Stuttgart, 1973.

Reaman, G. Elmore. "The Diary of a German on his Way to Upper Canada," *The American German Review,* XIX:5 (1953), 27-29.

St. John's Evangelical Church, Snyder, Ontario. *Historical Sketch of St. John's Evangelical Church, 1834-1934.* Stevensville, 1934.

Wadel, Viola R. "The German Lutheran Settlement of Rainham Township, County of Haldimand, Ontario," *German-Canadian Yearbook,* VIII (1984), 129-132.

CHAPTER XXIV: THE PENNSYLVANIA GERMAN MENNONITE MIGRATIONS

Baumann, Paul S. "The Unchanging Old Order Mennonites," *German-Canadian Yearbook,* III (1976), 97-105.

Burkholder, Lewis J. *A Brief History of the Mennonites in Ontario.* Toronto, 1935.

Burkholder, L.J. "The Early Mennonite Settlements in Ontario," *The Mennonite Quarterly Review,* V:8 (1934), 103-122.

Cassel, Daniel R. *Geschichte der Mennoniten.* Philadelphia, 1890.

Dunham, Mabel. *Grand River.* Toronto, 1945.

Eby, Ezra E. *A Biographical History of Waterloo Township and Other Townships in the County: Early Settlers and Their Descendants.* Berlin, Ont., 1895.

Epp, Frank H. *Mennonites in Canada, 1786-1920: The History of a Separate People.* Toronto, 1974.

Gingerich, Melvin. *Mennonite Attire Through Four Centuries.* Breinigsville, Pa., 1970.

Gingerich, Orlando. *The Amish of Canada.* Waterloo, 1972.

Horst, Isaac R. *Separate and Peculiar.* N.P., 1979.

Horst, Isaac R. *Thou Art Peter: A Story of the Pioneer Peter Martin and the Woolwich Mennonites.* Mt. Forest, Ont., 1983.

Horst, Isaac R. *Up the Conestogo.* Mt. Forest, Ont., 1979.

Hostetler, John A. *Amish Society.* Baltimore, 1963.

Lohmann, Martin. *Die Bedeutung der deutschen Ansiedlungen in Pennsylvanien.* Stuttgart, 1923.

Reaman, G. Elmore. *The Trail of the Black Walnut.* Toronto, 1957.

CHAPTER XXV: THE UNITED EMPIRE LOYALISTS

Bausenhart, Werner A. "Factors Contributing to the Assimilation of the German United Loyalists of the Upper St. Lawrence and the Bay of Quinté," *German Canadian Studies Annals,* 5 (1985), 20-31.

Bausenhart, Werner. *German Immigration and Assimilation in Ontario 1783-1918.* Ottawa, 1989.

Beacock Fryer, Mary. "Captain John Walden Meyers: Loyalist Spy," *German-Canadian Yearbook,* II (1975), 70-82.

Bell, David V.J. "The Loyalist Tradition in Canada," in J.M. Bumstead, ed. *Canadian History Before Confederation: Essays and Interpretations.* Georgetown, 1979, 209-226.

Benton, Nathaniel S. *History of Herkimer County Including the Upper Mohawk Valley From the Earliest Period to the Present Time.* Albany, 1865.

Brite, John Duncan. "The Attitude of European States Toward Emigration to the American Colonies and the United States, 1607-1820." Ph.D. thesis, University of Chicago, 1937.

Crewe, R. James, Jenifer A. Ludbrook, Daniel Francis. *Living in North America.* Toronto, 1986.

Cronmiller, Carl R. *A History of the Lutheran Church in Canada.* Vol. 1. Toronto, 1961.

Fryer, Mary Beacock. "Captain John Walden Meyers: Loyalist Spy," *German-Canadian Yearbook,* II (1975), 70-82.

Fryer, Mary Beacock. *Loyalist Spy: The Experiences of Captain John Walden Meyers During the American Revolution.* Brockville, Ont., 1974.

Fryer, Mary Beacock. "The Remarkable Hecks," *German-Canadian Yearbook,* IV (1978), 63-73.

Häberle, Daniel. *Auswanderung und Koloniegründungen der Pfälzer im 18. Jahrhundert.* Kaiserslautern, 1909.

Hansen, Marcus Lee. *The Mingling of the Canadian and American Peoples.* Toronto, 1940.

Hawn, Dexter. "Loyalist Descendants of a 1709 Palatine Emigrant Family in Ontario, 1784. A 75-Year Journey from Dienheim (Germany) to Cornwall (Canada) via Holland, England and the Hudson and Schoharie Valley Settlements in the United States," *German-Canadian Yearbook,* VIII (1984), 115-124.

Hawn, Dexter. "'Palatines' und deren Nachkommen unter den Loyalisten in Kanada." *Canadiana Germanica, Occasional Papers,* Nr.4 (1983).

Hutton, John. "St. Catherines, Ontario: For Jacob Dittrick, a First Settler, it was a Link with the Past," *German-Canadian Yearbook,* VIII (1984), 125-132.

Knittle, Walter Allen. *Early Eighteenth Century Palatine Emigration: A British Government Redemptioner Project to Manufacture Naval Stores.* Baltimore, 1965.

MacKinnon, Neil. *This Unfriendly Soil: The Loyalist Experience in Nova Scotia, 1783-1791.* Kingston and Montreal, 1986.

Magee, Joan. *Loyalist Mosaic: A Multi-ethnic Heritage.* Toronto and Charlottetown, 1984.

Mika, Nick and Helma. *United Empire Loyalists: Pioneers of Upper Canada.* Belleville, Ont., 1976.

Piro, Rolf A. "Die Bahls (the Ball Family): Das Wirken und das Erbe einer Empire-Loyalist Familie in Niagara," *German-Canadian Yearbook,* IV (1978), 127-134.

Piro, Rolf A. "German-Speaking Missionaries and Soldiers Among the Indians of Upper and Lower Canada," *German-Canadian Yearbook,* V (1979), 25-35.

Raeman, G. Elmore. *The Trail of the Black Walnut.* Toronto, 1957.

Rupp, August. *Pfälzische Kolonisation in Nordamerika.* Stuttgart, 1938.

Trautz, Fritz. *Die Pfälzische Auswanderung nach Nordamerika im 18. Jahrhundert.* Heidelberg, 1959.

Wallace, W.S. "The Overland Loyalists," *The Canadian Magazine,* XLIII:6 (October 1914), 573-577.

Weissenborn, Georg K. "Johann Samuel Schwerdtfeger: the Saint of the St. Lawrence Seaway (1734-1803)," *German-Canadian Yearbook,* II (1975), 189-192.

CHAPTER XXVI: THE HESSIANS

Arndt, Karl J.R. "Die Reise der Braunschweigischen Hülfstruppen nach Quebec im Jahre 1776 und die Folgen," *Annalen Deutschkanadische Studien,* 2 (1978), 1-3.

Atwood, Rodney. *The Hessians: Mercenaries from Hessen-Kassel in the American Revolution.* Cambridge, 1980.

Barrett, Beryl. "The Early Hessian Settlers of Prince Edward Island," *Journal of the Johannes Schwalm Historical Association, Inc.,* II:2 (1982), 1-12.

Blue, Charles S. "The German Legion in Canada," *The Canadian Magazine of Politics, Science, Art and Literature,* XLIV:3, (January 1915), 229-238.

Caux, Arthur. "Les colons allemands de Saint Gilles et leurs descendants dans Lotbinière," *Bulletin des recherches historiques,* 57 (1951), 50-60.

Cooper, John Erwin. "Three German Military Officers and Canada," *German-Canadian Yearbook,* IV (1978), 57-62.

Cronau, Rudolf. *Drei Jahrhunderte deutschen Lebens in Amerika: Eine Geschichte der Deutschen in den Vereinigten Staaten.* Berlin, 1909.

Cronmiller, Carl R. *A History of the Lutheran Church in Canada.* Vol. 1. Toronto, 1961.

Debor, Herbert Wilhelm. "German Regiments in Canada, 1776-1783. Part I," *German-Canadian Yearbook,* II (1975), 34-49.

Debor, Herbert Wilhelm. "German Soldiers of the American War of Independence as Settlers in Canada," *German-Canadian Yearbook,* III (1976), 71-93.

Debor, H.W. "Sie kamen nicht mit leeren Händen...," *Manitoba Courier,* February 16, 1961.

DeMarce, Virginia Easley. *The Settlement of Former German Auxiliary Troops in Canada After the American Revolution.* Arlington, Va., 1984.

Faust, Albert Bernhardt. *The German Element in the United States.* Vol. I. New York, 1927.

Forbes, Esther. *Paul Revere and the World He Lived In.* Boston, 1942.

Gradish, Stephen Francis. "The German Mercenaries in Canada, 1776-1783," M.A. thesis, University of Western Ontario, 1964.

Gürttler, Karin. "Das Trestlerhaus geht einer ungewissen Zukunft entgegen," *Canadiana Germanica,* 40 (1983), 1-5.

Hess, Anna K. "A Voyage of Duty: the Riedesels in America," *German-Canadian Yearbook,* I (1973), 131-139.

Hitsman, J. Mackay. *Safeguarding Canada, 1763-1871.* Toronto, 1968.

Kapp, Friedrich. *Der Soldatenhandel deutscher Fürsten nach Amerika (1775-1783).* Berlin, 1874.

Kipping, Ernst. *The Hessian View of America, 1776-1783.* Monmouth Beach, N.J., 1971.

Kipping, Ernst. *Die Truppen von Hessen-Kassel im Amerikanischen Unabhängigkeitskrieg, 1776-1783.* Darmstadt, 1965.

Kügler, Dietmar. *Die deutschen Truppen im amerikanischen Unabhängigkeitskrieg, 1775-1783.* Stuttgart, 1980.

Löher, Franz. *Geschichte und Zustände der Deutschen in Amerika.* Göttingen, 1855.

Lowell, Edward J. *The Hessians and Other German Auxiliaries of Great Britain in the Revolutionary War.* New York, 1884.

MacKinnon, Neil. *This Unfriendly Soil: The Loyalist Experience in Nova Scotia, 1783-1791.* Kingston and Montreal, 1986.

Mika, Nick and Helma. *United Empire Loyalists: Pioneers of Upper Canada.* Belleville, Ont., 1976.

Punch, Terrence M. "Vieth (Veith), Adolphus Christoph," *Dictionary of Canadian Biography,* VI (1978).

Seguin, Robert-Lionel. "L'apport germanique dans le peuplement de Vaudreuil et Soulanges," *Bulletin des recherches historiques,* 63 (1957), 42-58.

Teuscher, Gerhart, ed. *DuRoy, Anton Adolf. Tagebuch der Seereise von Stade nach Quebec in Amerika 1776.* Toronto, 1983.

Wilhelmy, Jean-Pierre. *German Mercenaries in Canada.* Beloeil, 1985.

Zimmermann, Lothar. "It's a long way to Quebec: An Episode Relating to the North American Campaign of the Knyphausen Regiment," *German-Canadian Yearbook,* VI (1981), 28-41.

Zimmermann, Lothar, ed. *Vertrauliche Briefe aus Kanada und Neuengland vom J. 1777 und 1778, Aus Herrn Prof. Schlözer's Briefwechsel.* Toronto, 1981.

CHAPTER XXVII: THE MORAVIANS

Allen, Walser H. *Who are the Moravians? The Story of the Moravian Church, a World-Wide Fellowship.* Bethlehem, Pa., 1981.

Bassler, Gerhard P. "Silent Heritage: Four Centuries of Germans in Newfoundland and Labrador," unpublished manuscript.

Bittinger, Lucy Forney. *The Germans in Colonial Times.* New York, 1901.

Brice-Bennett, Carol. "Two Opinions: Inuit and Moravian Missionaries in Labrador, 1804-1860," M.A. thesis, Memorial University of Newfoundland, 1981.

Brock, Daniel J. "Zeisberger, David," *Dictionary of Canadian Biography,* V (1983).

Hiller, J.K. "The Foundation and the Early Years of the Moravian Mission in Labrador, 1752-1805," M.A. thesis, Memorial University of Newfoundland, 1967.

Hiller, J.K. "The Moravians in Labrador, 1771-1805," *The Polar Record,* XV:99 (1971), 839-854.

Jannasch, Hans Windekilde. *Erziehung zur Freiheit: Ein Lebensbericht.* Göttingen, 1970.

Jannasch, Hans Windekilde. *Unter Hottentotten und Eskimos: Das Leben meines Vaters.* Lüneburg, 1950.

Macpherson, Alan G. "Early Moravian Interest in Northern Labrador Weather and Climate: The Beginning of Instrumental Recording in Newfoundland," in Donald H. Steele, ed. *Early Science in Newfoundland and Labrador.* St. John's, 1987, 30-41.

Payne, Robert, ed. *The White Arctic: Case Studies from the Labrador Coast.* St. John's, 1985.

Peacock, F.W. "Languages in Contact in Labrador," in William Kirwin, ed. *Regional Language Studies -- Newfoundland,* 5 (January 1974), 1-8.

Peacock, F.W. "The Moravian Mission in Labrador," *Canadian Geographical Journal,* 75:5 (May 1960), 182-189.

Peacock, F.W. "The Moravian Mission in Labrador, 1752-1979: The Goodly Heritage." Unpublished book manuscript, 1980.

Ratz, Alfred E. "Frühe Kulturarbeit deutscher Herrnhuter in Labrador," *German-Canadian Yearbook,* II (1975), 50-69.

Scheffel, David. "The Demographic Consequences of European Contact with Labrador Inuit," M.A. thesis, Memorial University of Newfoundland, 1980.

Schulze, Adolf. *Abriß einer Geschichte der Brüdermission.* Herrnhut, 1901.

Stolz, J.W. "Bibliographie der naturwissenschaftlichen Arbeiten aus dem Kreise der Brüdergemeinde," *Zeitschrift für Brüdergeschichte,* 10 (1916), 89-127.

Taylor, J. Garth. *Labrador Eskimo Settlements of the Early Contact Period.* Ottawa, 1974.

Weissenborn, Georg K. "David Zeisberger: The Apostle of the Indians," *German-Canadian Yearbook,* II (1975), 185-188.

Whiteley, William H. "Erhardt, John Christian," *Dictionary of Canadian Biography,* III (1974).

Whiteley, William H. "The Establishment of the Moravian Mission in Labrador and British Policy, 1763-83," *The Canadian Historical Review,* XXXIII (March 1964), 29-50.

Whiteley, William H. "The Moravian Missionaries and the Labrador Eskimos in the Eighteenth Century," *Church History,* XXXV:1 (1966), 3-19.

Wilson, E., ed. *With the Harmony to Labrador.* N.p., [1970s?].

CHAPTER XXVIII: THE LUNENBURG GERMANS

Arndt, Karl J.R., ed. "Halifax and Lunenburg in 1782, or Halle and London as Sources of German-Canadian Research," *German-Canadian Yearbook,* IV (1978). 114-121.

Artiss, David. "German Cultural Heritage Studies in Atlantic Canada," in Rainer Hempel, ed. *Proceedings of the Atlantic University Teachers of German Conference.* Sackville, 1979, 72-82.

Beck, J. Murray. "Jessen, Dettlieb (Detleff) Christopher," *Dictionary of Canadian Biography,* Vol.V (1983).

Beck, J. Murray. "Knaut, Philip Augustus," *Dictionary of Canadian Biography,* Vol. IV (1979).

Beck, Murray. "Rudolf, William," *Dictionary of Canadian Biography,* Vol. VIII (1985).

Bell, Winthrop Pickard. *The 'Foreign Protestants' and the Settlement of Nova Scotia: The History of a Piece of Arrested British Colonial Policy in the Eighteenth Century.* Toronto, 1961.

Bohlmann, Ursula. "The Germans: The Protestant Buffer," in Douglas F. Campbell, ed. *Banked Fires: The Ethnics of Nova Scotia.* Port Credit, Ont., 1978.

Bourinot, John G. *Builders of Nova Scotia: A Historical Review.* Toronto, 1900.

Creighton, Helen. *Folklore of Lunenburg County, Nova Scotia.* Ottawa, 1950.

Debor, Herbert Wilhelm. "Early German Immigration in Nova Scotia," *German-Canadian Yearbook,* I (1973), 67-70.

DesBrisay, Mather Byles. *History of the County of Lunenburg.* Toronto, 1895.

Froeschle, Hartmut. "Der 'Neu-Schottländische Calender" (Halifax, 1788-1801)," *German Canadian Studies Annals,* 4 (1983), 73-96.

Haliburton, Thomas Chandler. *An Historical and Statistical Account of Nova Scotia.* Halifax, 1929.

Lehmann, Heinz. *The German Canadians, 1750-1937: Immigration, Settlement and Culture.* St. John's, 1986.

Lochhead, Douglas G. "Henry, Anthony (also Anton Heinrich or Henrich)," *Dictionary of Canadian Biography,* Vol. IV (1979).

Makay, Donald C. "Etter, Benjamin," *Dictionary of Canadian Biography,* Vol. VI (1987).

Mackay, Donald C. "Nordbeck, Peter," *Dictionary of Canadian Biography,* Vol. IX (1976).

MacKenzie, A.A. "Zouberbuhler, Sebastian," *Dictionary of Canadian Biography,* Vol. IV (1979).

McCreath, Peter L. and John G. Leefe. *History of Early Nova Scotia.* Tantallon, N.S., 1982.

McNutt, W.S. *The Atlantic Provinces: The Emergence of Colonial Society, 1712-1857.* Toronto, 1965.

Nightingale, Marie. *Out of Old Nova Scotia Kitchens: A collection of traditional recipes of Nova Scotia and the story of the people who cooked them.* Halifax, 1970.

Pross, Catherine. "Schwartz, Otto William," *Dictionary of Canadian Biography,* Vol. IV (1979).

Punch, Terrence M. "Vieth (Veith), Adolphus Christoph," *Dictionary of Canadian Biography,* Vol. VI (1978).

Rawlyk, G.A. "Waldo, Samuel," *Dictionary of Canadian Biography,* Vol. III (1974)

Richter, Manfred. "Christmas and New Year's Customs among the German Canadians in Lunenburg County, Nova Scotia," *German Canadian Studies Annals,* 4 (1983), 97-109.

Richter, Manfred. "Die deutsche Mundart von Lunenburg County, Nova Scotia: Ein Überblick," *German Canadian Studies Annals,* 2 (1978), 19-30.

Rompkey, Ronald. "Erad (originally Ehrhard), Johann Burghard," *Dictionary of Canadian Biography,* Vol. III (1974).

Rompkey, Ronald, ed. *Expeditions of Honour: The Journal of John Salusbury in Halifax, Nova Scotia, 1749-53.* Newark, London and Toronto, 1982.

Sautter, Udo. "Die Lunenburg Deutschen," *German Canadian Studies Annals,* 1 (1976), 70-85.

Sautter, Udo. "Ein deutscher Geistlicher in Neuschottland: Johann Adam Moschell (1795-1849)," *German-Canadian Yearbook,* I (1973), 153-160.

Taubert, Sigfred. "The First German Printers in Canada," *German-Canadian Yearbook,* I (1973), 71-75.

Waseem, Gertrud. "Die Fahrt nach Nova Scotia: Zur Vorgeschichte der Gründung Lunenburgs, N.S.," *German-Canadian Yearbook,* III (1976), 140-159.

Waseem, Gertrud. "Neue Heimat in fremdem Land: Zur Geschichte der Gründung Lunenburgs, N.S.," *German-Canadian Yearbook,* IV (1978), 74-92.

CHAPTER XXIX: EARLY QUEBEC

Bonnault, Claude de. "Les Suisses au Canada," *Le Bulletin de recherches historiques,* 61 (1955), 51-70.

Bovay, E.H. *Le Canada et les Suisses 1604-1974.* Fribourg, 1976.

Brite, John Duncan. "The Attitude of European States Toward Emigration to the American Colonies and the United States, 1607-1820," Ph.D. thesis, University of Chicago, 1937.

Cooper, John Irwin. "Three German Military Officers and Canada," *German-Canadian Yearbook,* IV (1978), 57-62.

Cyr, Céline. "Wurtele, Josias," *Dictionary of Canadian Biography,* Vol. VI (1987).

Debor, H.W. *1664-1964: Die Deutschen in der Provinz Québec.* Montréal, 1963.

Debor, H.W. "Württemberger standen an der Wiege der Deutschen Gesellschaft Montreal," *Montreal-Courier,* January 25, 1962.

Derome, Robert. "Arnoldi, Michael," *Dictionary of Canadian Biography,* Vol.V (1983).

Derome, Robert. "Schindler, Joseph (Jonas)," *Dictionary of Canadian Biography,* Vol. IV (1979).

Douville, Raymond. "Gugy, Conrad," *Dictionary of Canadian Biography,* Vol. IV (1979).

German Society Montréal, 1835-1985. *German Canadian Artists in Québec.* Montréal, 1985.

Graffenried, Friedrich von. "Sechs Jahre in Canada, 1813-1819," *Jahresbericht der Geographischen Gesellschaft in Bern,* 10 (1890), 73-138.

Hitsman, J. Mackay. *The Incredible War of 1812.* Toronto, 1965.

Hitsman, J. Mackay. *Safeguarding Canada, 1763-1871.* Toronto, 1968.

Jaenen, Cornelius J. "Ethnic Studies: An Integral Part of Canadian Studies," in W. Isajiw, ed. *Identities: The Impact of Ethnicity on Canadian Society.* Toronto, 1977, xi-xvii.

Jaenen, Cornelius J. "Problems of Assimilation in New France," *French Historical Studies,* 4 (1966), 265-289.

Lach, Friedhelm. "Deutschkanadische Kunst in Québec," *Annalen Deutschkanadische Studien,* V (1985), 125-132.

Luethy, Ivor C.E. "General Sir Frederick Haldimand: A Swiss Governor General of Canada," *Canadian Ethnic Studies,* III (1971), 63-75.

Milne, A.T. "Haldimand, Peter Frederick," *Dictionary of Canadian Biography,* Vol. III (1974).

Momryk, M. "Ermatinger, Lawrence," *Dictionary of Canadian Biography,* Vol. IV (1979).

Parkman, F. *Montcalm and Wolfe.* Boston, 1925.

Plante, Hermann. "Arnoldi, Phebe (rebaptized Appoline, named de Sainte-Angèle Diehl)," *Dictionary of Canadian Biography,* Vol. VI (1987).

Schweizer, Leo, ed. *1874-1974 Swiss National Society Montreal.* Montreal, 1984.

Sutherland, Stuart R.J. Pierre Tousignant and Madeleine Dionne-Tousignant. "Haldimand, Sir Frederick," *Dictionary of Canadian Biography,* Vol.V (1983), 887-904.

Turnbull, J.R. "Dieskau, Jean-Armand (Johan Herman?), Baron de Dieskau," *Dictionary of Canadian Biography,* Vol. III (1974).

Turner, W.B. "Rottenburg, Francis (Franz) De, Baron de Rottenburg," *Dictionary of Canadian Biography,* Vol. VI (1987).

Weissenborn, Georg K. "Johann Daniel Arnoldi. The Pioneer Doctor of Lower Canada (1774-1849)," *German-Canadian Yearbook,* IV (1978), 254-256.

CHAPTER XXX: NEWFOUNDLAND

Bassler, Gerhard P. "The German Experience in Newfoundland to 1914: Migrations, Connections, Images," *German Canadian Studies Annals,* 7 (1991).

Bassler, Gerhard P. "Germans and German Connections in Newfoundland to 1914," *Newfoundland Quarterly,* LXXXVI:3 (Spring 1991), 18-26.

Bassler, Gerhard P. "Silent Heritage: Four Centuries of Germans in Newfoundland and Labrador," unpublished manuscript.

Brandt, Armin M. *Bau deinen Altar auf fremder Erde. Die Deutschen in Amerika: 300 Jahre Germantown.* Stuttgart, 1983.

Debor, H.W. *1664-1964: Die Deutschen in der Provinz Quebec.* Montreal, 1963.

Hennings, C.R. *Deutsche in England.* Stuttgart, 1923.

Ingstad, Anne Stine. *The Discovery of a Norse Settlement in America: Excavations at L'Anse aux Meadows, Newfoundland, 1961-1968.* Oslo, 1977.

Ingstad, Helge. *The Norse Discovery of America: The Historical Background and the Evidence of the Norse Settlement Discovered in Newfoundland.* Oslo, 1985.

Ingstad, Helge. *Westward to Vinland: The Discovery of Pre-Columbian Norse House-sites in North America.* Toronto, 1969.

Ingstad, Helge. "Vinland Ruins Prove Vikings Found the New World," *National Geographic,* 147:11 (November 1964), 709-734.

Jones, Frederick and G.M. Story. "Anspach, Lewis Amadeus," *Dictionary of Canadian Biography,* Vol.VI (1987).

Jones, Gwyn. *The Norse Atlantic Saga: Being the Norse Voyages of Discovery and Settlement to Iceland, Greenland, America.* London, 1964.

Larsen, Sofus. *The Discovery of North America Twenty Years Before Columbus.* Copenhagen and London, 1925.

Larson, Lawrence M. "Did John Scolvus Visit Labrador and Newfoundland In or About 1476?" in J.R. Smallwood, ed. *The Book of Newfoundland, Vol. VI.* St. John's, 1975, 445-449.

Lindsay, Charles. "Was L'Anse aux Meadows a Norse Outpost?" *Canadian Geographical Journal,* 92:1 (1977), 36-43.

Lounsbury, Ralph Greenlee. *The British Fishery at Newfoundland, 1634-1763.* New Haven, 1934.

Luttrell, Narcissus. *A Brief Historical Relation of State Affairs from September 1678 to April 1714.* Oxford, 1857.

Morison, Samuel Eliot. *The European Discovery of America: The Northern Voyages AD 500-1600.* New York, 1971.

Prowse, D.W. *A History of Newfoundland from the English, Colonial and Foreign Records.* London and New York, 1895.

Quinn, David B., ed. *Newfoundland from Fishery to Colony. Northwest Passage Searches. Vol. IV.* New York, 1979.

Quinn, David B. *The Voyages and Colonial Enterprises of Sir Humphrey Gilbert. Vol. I.* London, 1940.

Rowse, A.L. *The England of Elizabeth.* London, 1953.

Sturtevant, W.C. "The first Inuit depiction by Europeans," *Etudes Inuit Studies,* IV:1-2 (1980), 47-49.

Sturtevant, William C. "First Visual Images of Native America," in Fredi Chiapelli, ed. *First Images of America: The Impact of the New World on the Old. Vol.I.* Berkeley, 1976, 417-453.

Tuckermann, Walter. "Der deutsche Anteil an derErschliessung und Erforschung Nordamerikas," *Zeitschrift für Erdkunde,* 8 (1940), 363-374.

Uebe, Richard. *Labrador: Eine physiographische und kulturgeographische Skizze.* Halle, 1909.

Wahlgren, Erik. *The Vikings and America.* London, 1986.

Wallace, Brigitte. "Further Developments in Research on Native and Norse Occupations at L'Anse aux Meadows, Nfld," Paper presented at the Annual Meeting of the Canadian Archeological Association in Hamilton, Ontario, May 1, 1982.